PEOPLE'S BIBLE COMMENTARY

HAGGAI ZECHARIAH MALACHI

ERIC S. HARTZELL

PBC

CONCORDIA PUBLISHING HOUSE · SAINT LOUIS

Revised edition first printed in 2005.
Copyright © 1994 Concordia Publishing House
3558 S. Jefferson Ave., St. Louis, MO 63118-3968
1-800-325-3040 · www.cph.org

Commentary and pictures are reprinted from HAGGAI/ ZECHARIAH/MALACHI (The People's Bible Series), copyright © 1991 by Northwestern Publishing House. Used by permission.

Interior illustrations by Glenn Myers.

Unless otherwise stated, the Scripture quotations in this publication are taken from the HOLY BIBLE, NEW INTERNATIONAL VERSION®. NIV®. Copyright © 1973, 1978, 1984 by International Bible Society. Used by permission of Zondervan Publishing House. All rights reserved.

Manufactured in the United States of America

ISBN 0-7586-0438-6

1 2 3 4 5 6 7 8 9 10   14 13 12 11 10 09 08 07 06 05

CONTENTS

ILLUSTRATIONS

EDITOR'S PREFACE

The *People's Bible Commentary* is just what the name implies—a Bible and commentary for the people. It includes the complete text of the Holy Scriptures in the popular New International Version. The commentary following the Scripture sections contains personal applications as well as historical background and explanations of the text.

The authors of the *People's Bible Commentary* are men of scholarship and practical insight gained from years of experience in the teaching and preaching ministries. They have tried to avoid the technical jargon which limits so many commentary series to professional Bible scholars.

The most important feature of these books is that they are Christ-centered. Speaking of the Old Testament Scriptures, Jesus himself declared, "These are the Scriptures that testify about me" (John 5:39). Each volume of the *People's Bible Commentary* directs our attention to Jesus Christ. He is the center of the entire Bible. He is our only Savior.

We dedicate these volumes to the glory of God and to the good of his people.

The Publishers

INTRODUCTION TO HAGGAI

Historical background

The Old Testament book of Ezra provides the historical setting for the book of Haggai. To understand God's people as Haggai knew them and talked to them, we must first hear what Ezra tells us.

The Jews had just come from 70 years of captivity under the Neo-Babylonian Empire (Kings Nebuchadnezzar through Belshazzar). In 539 B.C. Cyrus, king of the Medes (Persians), ended the Neo-Babylonian Empire. He came at night when King Belshazzar was having a drunken feast and handwriting appeared on the wall: MENE, MENE, TEKEL, PARSIN. "God has numbered the days of your reign and brought it to an end" (Daniel 5:26).

But it was not until 535 B.C. that the captivity actually came to an end. Ezra 1:1 tells us, "In the first year of Cyrus king of Persia, in order to fulfill the word of the LORD spoken by Jeremiah, the LORD moved the heart of Cyrus king of Persia to make a proclamation throughout his realm and to put it in writing."

God's people were to go back home. When they arrived, the work on the temple began. "When they arrived at the house of the LORD in Jerusalem, some of the heads of the families gave freewill offerings toward the rebuilding of the house of God on its site" (Ezra 2:68). "Despite their

1

fear of the peoples around them, they built the altar on its foundation and sacrificed burnt offerings on it to the LORD" (Ezra 3:3).

The rebuilding began outwardly with good success. "They gave money to the masons and carpenters, and gave food and drink and oil to the people of Sidon and Tyre, so that they would bring cedar logs by sea from Lebanon to Joppa, as authorized by Cyrus king of Persia. In the second month of the second year after their arrival at the house of God in Jerusalem, Zerubbabel son of Shealtiel, Jeshua son of Jozadak and the rest of their brothers . . . began the work" (Ezra 3:7,8).

Even though things appeared to be getting under way and the foundation was laid, something was wrong. "Many of the older priests and Levites and family heads, who had seen the former temple, wept aloud when they saw the foundation of this temple being laid, while many others shouted for joy. No one could distinguish the sound of the shouts of joy from the sound of weeping, because the people made so much noise" (Ezra 3:12,13).

The Old Testament commentator C. F. Keil ventures the following as a reason why some were weeping: "This weeping can hardly be explained merely from the recollection of the trials and sufferings of the last fifty years, which came involuntarily into their mind at that moment of solemn rejoicing, but was no doubt occasioned chiefly by the sight of the miserable circumstances under which the congregation took this work in hand."

Work began on the temple in 536 B.C. It never came to completion. The prophet Haggai tells us why. It wasn't that there were enemies and frustrations to the plan for rebuilding. The Samaritans certainly opposed the building plans, but it was sin, not the Samaritans, that kept God's house unfinished.

The people were more interested in their own houses than in God's house. Ezra 5:1 tells us, "Haggai the prophet and Zechariah the prophet, a descendant of Iddo, prophesied to the Jews in Judah and Jerusalem in the name of the God of Israel, who was over them." In view of the flagging efforts the prophets saw, their message was, "Build God's house!"

This is the theme of the book of Haggai.

Why all this importance placed on the building of God's house? This is the question that Haggai's people no doubt muttered under their breaths. The question still spooks around among modern-day Christians.

For the Old Testament believers, the temple was the place where God chose to dwell in a special manner. There his name resided. There his people gathered, and he met them and talked to them in a special way. The Lord had pointed to Solomon and said, "He is the one who will build a house for my Name" (2 Samuel 7:13). The temple was set up as a vital link between God and his people. "As for this temple you are building, if you follow my decrees, carry out my regulations and keep all my commands and obey them, I will fulfill through you the promise I gave to David your father. And I will live among the Israelites and will not abandon my people Israel" (1 Kings 6:12,13).

When the temple was dedicated, God kept his promise: "I have heard the prayer and plea you have made before me; I have consecrated this temple, which you have built, by putting my Name there forever. My eyes and my heart will always be there" (1 Kings 9:3).

Although we, in the New Testament time, do not worship in a temple, we still have a place that we call God's house. It is our church. And regardless of the time in history, one can always tell something about the believers by looking at their house of worship. If they expect their God to live in a shack,

3

something is wrong, especially when the people themselves live in fine houses.

Haggai's concern was that his people put their God first and themselves second. This remains our concern today. This is, in fact, the First Commandment: "You shall have no other gods." This emphasis is what makes this little book in the Old Testament still so important for us today.

Outline

Take care of God's house.

I.   The first word from the Lord, a warning (1:1-11), and the people's response (1:12-15).

II. The second word from the Lord, a word of encouragement (2:1-9).

III. The third word from the Lord, a word of concern (2:10-18) and a promise (2:19).

IV. The fourth word from the Lord, a word of comfort to the ruler (2:20-23).

PART ONE

The First Word from the Lord
(1:1-15)

A warning

1 **In the second year of King Darius, on the first day of the
sixth month, the word of the LORD came through the prophet
Haggai to Zerubbabel son of Shealtiel, governor of Judah, and to
Joshua son of Jehozadak, the high priest:**

**²This is what the LORD Almighty says: "These people say, 'The
time has not yet come for the LORD's house to be built.'"**

**³Then the word of the LORD came through the prophet Hag-
gai: ⁴"Is it a time for you yourselves to be living in your paneled
houses, while this house remains a ruin?"**

**⁵Now this is what the LORD Almighty says: "Give careful
thought to your ways. ⁶You have planted much, but have har-
vested little. You eat, but never have enough. You drink, but
never have your fill. You put on clothes, but are not warm. You
earn wages, only to put them in a purse with holes in it."**

The Bible is a historical book. It gives dates in time. God
appeared to the world "when the time had fully come" (Galatians 4:4). It is not legend from the hoary past that we find
recorded in the book of Haggai. In a remarkable way, God has
pinned down the occurrences of the Bible with secular history.

The beginning of the book demonstrates this. The Lord
took great care through the pen of the prophet Haggai
clearly and painstakingly to jot down the date for each of
the four "words" of the Lord that the book includes. The
book begins, "In the second year of King Darius [also
named Cyrus], on the first day of the sixth month, the word
of the LORD came through the prophet Haggai."

Temple in ruins

Some critics raise their eyebrows here. Ezra chapter 4, which speaks of the rebuilding of the temple and lists the men Zerubbabel and Jeshua, who clearly belong to our story, also mentions a letter written to Artaxerxes. This letter stemmed from an accusation made by the enemies of the Jews already at the time of Xerxes. Both Xerxes and Artaxerxes are mentioned. Then verse 24 at the end of the chapter says, "Thus the work on the house of God in Jerusalem came to a standstill until the second year of the reign of Darius king of Persia." The critics say this can't be right. The temple was known to have been completed under Darius, who most certainly reigned before both Xerxes and Artaxerxes.

We can explain the problem if we remember that Ezra was writing history. He lived at the time of Artaxerxes. By inspiration he wrote of all the resistance to God's people, not only the resistance against them when they rebuilt the temple, but also the resistance that leveled against their attempts to restore the wall around Jerusalem. From his viewpoint in history, Ezra knew of all the opposition and by God's direction included it in his story in chapter 4 even though chronologically it didn't fit.

The NIV obviously follows this idea when it sets off this section in Ezra chapter 4 as separate from the rest and entitles it, "Later Opposition under Xerxes and Artaxerxes."

The point of mentioning this "problem" is that as Bible believers we do not have to blush every time people find something historically askew (in their opinion). Just because we lack historical facts to prove something the Bible maintains does not prove that the Bible is wrong. Anyone who would try and state this argues from silence. And arguments from silence have been proven wrong time and time again. Not so long ago, people said that writing was not in practice at the time of Moses and that there were no Hittites. Archaeology has since proven both statements false. People did indeed write at the time of Moses, and there were indeed an ancient people called Hittites.

Haggai was a real historical character. He sat down to write his book at a certain instant in history. The word was spoken first to a people who were living actual lives with unique problems and dangers. As temporal creatures, we sit down on our couches, turn on our lamps, open our Bibles to the book of Haggai, and read. In just this same temporal, natural way, the book was written and spoken to God's people at the time of Haggai.

Verse 1 says, "The word of the LORD came through the prophet Haggai to Zerubbabel . . . , and to Joshua." This repeats God's way of dealing with the people in the Old Testament time. He chose prophets who spoke for him. They came to his people and said over and over again, "This is what the LORD says."

It was no easier for Zerubbabel and Joshua to believe that God was really talking to them than it is for us today to believe it when our pastors and teachers tell us, "This is what God says." When Zerubbabel and Joshua looked, they saw Haggai. They maybe knew him as a neighbor. He had peculiarities and traits like any other human being. He put his sandals on one at a time like any other person of his day. And it was this man who said, "This is what the Lord says." The remarkable thing is that Zerubbabel and Joshua believed that it was true! God was really talking! Verse 12 tells us, "Then Zerubbabel son of Shealtiel, Joshua son of Jehozadak, the high priest, and the whole remnant of the people obeyed the voice of the LORD their God and the message of the prophet Haggai, because the LORD their God had sent him."

This is the miracle of the sermon preached to God's people. A minister who is obviously a sinful human being stands before people and proclaims God's words, and the people believe! The apostle Paul marveled at this miracle too when he saw his people in Thessalonica. "We also thank God continually because, when you received the word of God, which you heard from us, you accepted it not as the word of men, but as it actually is, the word of God, which is at work in you who believe" (1 Thessalonians 2:13).

The people said, "The time has *not yet* come for the LORD's house to be built." This states the problem that Haggai faced with his people.

How easy it is to procrastinate with the Lord's concerns. How impressive the reasons for waiting. There was a strong force of Samaritans who frowned when they heard the word *temple*. In Ezra 4:2 we read that well-meaning locals came with this offer: "Let us help you build because, like you, we seek your God and have been sacrificing to him."

But the leaders answered, "You have no part with us in building a temple to our God" (Ezra 4:3). Too bad the Samaritans' doctrine was off. Too bad the leaders could not close their eyes to a few "minor" differences so that the people could have had help in the monumental task before them. Why not wait? Why senselessly antagonize the Persians? Why get reported to them as being so fanatical about matters of God as to build an impressive temple right out in the open? It would be better to keep the religion undercover. We better wait! After all, we have children to think of. The Persians have the nasty habit of impaling troublemakers on beams (Ezra 6:11).

The reasons for waiting were many. But perhaps the real reason the people waited is found in verse 4; in summary, the Lord is saying, "You aren't making my house because you are too busy making your own."

Now the problem has been distilled to a transgression of the First Commandment: "You shall have no other gods before me" (Exodus 20:3). This includes the smiling little god of personal convenience. It also includes the mirror-faced god, who always shows us ourselves when we worship him. The Lord says in a way not affected by time or culture, "Seek first his kingdom and his righteousness, and all these things will be given to you as well" (Matthew 6:33).

We spoke earlier of the weeping some of the people did when they saw how the temple was progressing. We spoke too of what one commentator surmised to be the reason. One thing is certain. Gone was the spirit of giving for the Lord's house that is mentioned in Moses' time: "The people are bringing more than enough for doing the work the LORD commanded to be done" (Exodus 36:5). Then Moses gave this order: "'No man or woman is to make anything else as an offering for the sanctuary.' And so the people were restrained from bringing more, because what they already had was more than enough to do all the work" (verses 6,7). Gone was the power to thrive in the face of opposition. Jonathan typified this strength when he spoke to his young armor-bearer: "Come, let's go over to the outpost of those uncircumcised fellows [the Philistines]. Perhaps the LORD will act in our behalf. Nothing can hinder the LORD from saving, whether by many or by few" (1 Samuel 14:6).

It is always a matter for weeping when God's people lose their determination and desire to establish his church and build his house. And the prophet must speak to us today. In the era of the greatest personal riches and per capita wealth that the world has ever seen and in a country that has been blessed with more material wealth than perhaps any country in history ever has been, the church goes begging. Building projects limp and stumble. Modest mission proposals languish. Even children learn to know what "budget crunch" means in the church. Can we claim that we have it harder than the exiles returning to Jerusalem? We too may be quick to say, "The time isn't right." But the Lord is equally quick in asking, "Is it a time for you yourselves to be living in your paneled houses, while this house remains a ruin?"

Verse 7 contains a phrase that will be repeated a number of times throughout the book: "Give careful thought to your ways." The Lord wants us to watch how we live. He wants us to evaluate what we do and then reevaluate. He holds us responsible for "our way."

The references in the Scripture to "the way" are legion. Solomon asserts in Proverbs, "When a man's ways are pleasing to the LORD, he makes even his enemies live at peace with him" (16:7). In that same chapter he adds, "There is a way that seems right to a man, but in the end it leads to death" (verse 25).

There is something else about this way. God's way for us isn't the natural way people live. In the matter of correct pathfinding, the Lord has to be the one to give us directions. "It is God who works in you to will and to act according to his good purpose" (Philippians 2:13). But as his children, our Father can and does tell us, "You watch your ways." Before the apostle Paul was converted on the road to Damascus, we read about him, "If he found any there who belonged to the Way, whether men or women, he might take them as prisoners to Jerusalem" (Acts 9:2). He knew he wasn't part of that "Way". But years later when he spoke to Felix the governor, he had changed: "I admit that I worship the God of our fathers as a follower of the Way" (Acts 24:14).

The Hebrew for the phrase "give careful thought to your ways" is literally "put your heart over your ways." We could also say, "Put your heart in your way." John offers the same advice in 1 John 3:18: "Dear children, let us not love with words or tongue but with actions and in truth." It is easy enough to say that we love Jesus, but does it look like it? One

11

way to tell is to look at the priorities we give his house and his work.

We need the blessing of putting God's house first!

It may be that God's people hedge because they cast long glances at their own financial needs and decide to skimp on God's house. In other words, people don't give and work for God as they should because they have the idea that by so doing they themselves will lack.

But as the Lord points out in verses 6 and 9 to 11, that idea backfires. The gist of what the Lord is saying in these verses is "The more you work for yourself, the less you will have. The more you work for God, the more you will have." Just look at what happens to people who panel their own houses and neglect God's. Harvests fail. Food and drink are in short supply. Clothes don't warm. Wages simply disappear. The purse has holes in it. Expectations vanish; God blows them away. There is drought and famine. The work of the hands is frustrated and fails.

⁷This is what the Lᴏʀᴅ Almighty says: "Give careful thought to your ways. ⁸Go up into the mountains and bring down timber and build the house, so that I may take pleasure in it and be honored," says the Lᴏʀᴅ. ⁹"You expected much, but see, it turned out to be little. What you brought home, I blew away. Why?" declares the Lᴏʀᴅ Almighty. "Because of my house, which remains a ruin, while each of you is busy with his own house. ¹⁰Therefore, because of you the heavens have withheld their dew and the earth its crops. ¹¹I called for a drought on the fields and the mountains, on the grain, the new wine, the oil and whatever the ground produces, on men and cattle, and on the labor of your hands."

The remedy for the bad things that happen to people who build their own houses at the expense of the Lord's house is in verse 8. "'Go up into the mountains and bring down timber and build the house, so that I may take pleasure in it and be honored,' says the LORD." Cutting the trees of Lebanon and getting them the one hundred plus miles to Jerusalem was backbreaking work. Besides being hard work, it was also costly and it took much time.

But there was a reason for all of the pains: "That I may take pleasure in it and be honored."

What an incentive to build God's house! It honors him! It is the expenditure of time, money, thought, and strength that lends worth to a gift. A gift of thousands of dollars that comes as an afterthought and does not even amount to the interest on the principal is not much of a gift in the eye of the receiver. On the other hand, a gift that may be in its sum total modest and unassuming to the outsider comes as a prize to the person who knows the work and effort that may stand behind it.

So it is with God's house. Our church may not be the grandest church building in the world. Our organization may not boast the most eloquent and gifted people on its roster. Our effort to preach and teach may not be carried out with finesse and beauty. But never mind that. It is God's house. We are the ones who call it that—and so does God. The people who go by on the outside do not call it God's house. It is beautiful regardless of the structure, if it was built in love. The Lord knows the motives of hearts.

He also knows a cold shoulder and an indifferent yawn. And he does something about these; everything goes to ruin. The misery comes "because of my house, which remains a ruin, while each of you is busy with his own house."

You can't get much clearer in your speech and insinuation than that. It is a judgment. We squirm under the accusation. We don't like it. But there it is! The only way we can get out of it is to be sure that we are putting God's house before our

13

own. "Seek first [the kingdom of God] and his righteousness, and all these things will be given to you" (Matthew 6:33).

There is nothing more important that a ruler (or pastor) can teach his people than this. With this as knowledge and practice, life prospers and is good. It is a sweeping promise. We must take God at his Word, both with regard to the warning and with regard to the promise.

A warning is perhaps in order here that we don't try to second guess the visible evidence and try to ascertain the crime. In other words, it isn't for us to judge every crop failure of a Christian farmer or every accident or setback a Christian might experience as some direct reference to unfaithfulness on that person's part or disregard for God's house and God's work. Job would be an example. Sometimes the Lord gives, and sometimes he takes away. Still in all, the blessing lies waiting. "I was young and now I am old, yet I have never seen the righteous forsaken or their children begging bread" (Psalm 37:25). And in Job's case we read that at the end of his suffering, the Lord blessed Job and gave him twice as much as he had before. The reason has a direct connection with the fact that in his life, Job put God first.

The people's response

¹²Then Zerubbabel son of Shealtiel, Joshua son of Jehozadak, the high priest, and the whole remnant of the people obeyed the voice of the LORD their God and the message of the prophet Haggai, because the LORD their God had sent him. And the people feared the LORD.

¹³Then Haggai, the LORD's messenger, gave this message of the LORD to the people: "I am with you," declares the LORD. ¹⁴So the LORD stirred up the spirit of Zerubbabel son of Shealtiel, governor of Judah, and the spirit of Joshua son of Jehozadak, the high priest, and the spirit of the whole remnant of the people. They came and began to work on the house of the LORD Almighty, their

God, ¹⁵on the twenty-fourth day of the sixth month in the second year of King Darius.

It is interesting to note the categories of people who responded to the Lord's command through the prophet. The people in the government responded: Zerubbabel son of Shealtiel. The people in the church responded: Joshua son of Jehozadak, the high priest. The people, the citizenry of the land, responded: "and the whole remnant of the people obeyed the voice of the Lord their God."

Israel was a theocracy. Still, the Lord used a governor. The history of God's people certainly shows the importance of a God-fearing leader. When the ruler feared God, the people prospered. When the ruler did not fear God, the people failed. Over and over again this seems to be the pattern—good leadership under God and there is prosperity; bad leadership where God is left out and the people languish.

Because of this fact, certainly a prayer that comes often from the Christian's heart is that the Lord would provide a godly government. Martin Luther incorporated this into his treatment of the Fourth Petition of the Lord's Prayer: "Daily bread includes everything that we need for our bodily welfare, such as . . . godly and faithful leaders, good government, good weather, peace and order, health, a good name, good friends, faithful neighbors, and the like."

When Governor Zerubbabel stepped forward to lead the rebuilding of God's house, it was a blessing. The governor heard God speaking to him; the priest heard God speaking to him; the layman heard God speaking to him. When God said, "Build my house," it was not just the church worker who was supposed to do it. The leader of the country was involved too—the executive and busy businessman. The people did not say, "Building God's house is the priest's business. That is his work; that is what we are paying him for."

When the people—all of them—heard the words of Haggai, they said, "This is the Lord talking." And we read, "The people feared the LORD."

This is what we referred to before as the miracle of a sermon. Haggai was an ordinary man, different only by virtue of his call. Yet the people said, "This isn't Haggai speaking. This is God himself. We had better listen." In verse 13 the Lord is quick to say, "I am with you." That is his name. Immanuel— God is with us. He wants to make his dwelling with us. He stands at the door and knocks. His work is not easy. There will be godless opposition, but our God is on our side! He tells us to be strong and work. He is with us!

He stirred up the spirits of the people. Once again in verse 14 each class of people is mentioned as being "stirred up." The Lord works in us to will and to do his good pleasure. We certainly do not have that dynamic spark by ourselves. It does not lie sheltered somewhere in our bosoms, ready to ignite the whole course of our lives on fire for God and for his house.

This spark that will quickly burn its way to the surface of our lives is a spark that we, unfortunately, have the power to extinguish. Stephen told his audience: "You stiff-necked people, with uncircumcised hearts and ears! You are just like your fathers: You always resist the Holy Spirit!" (Acts 7:51).

God works in kind. His Spirit works with our spirits, stirring them up. Spirit to spirit. It was that way already in Moses' day. "Moses said to the Israelites, 'See, the LORD has chosen Bezalel son of Uri, the son of Hur, of the tribe of Judah, and he has filled him with the Spirit of God, with skill, ability and knowledge in all kinds of crafts . . . And he has given both him and Oholiab son of Ahisamach, of the tribe of Dan, the ability to teach others'" (Exodus 35:30-34).

This is the thrill of watching God's church in action. He supplies the gifts to the people in the church. He puts the spirit in them to do the work. The people don't all have the same gifts, but together they build the church. They all complement one another. They all give evidence of the fact that the same Spirit is at work in them, stirring them into action.

"They came and began to work on the house of the LORD Almighty, their God." The sermon had its proper effect. The people heard and did something. This is loving God not only in words but in actions and in truth.

PART TWO

The Second Word from the Lord
(2:1-9)

A word of encouragement

2 On the twenty-first day of the seventh month, the word of the Lord came through the prophet Haggai: ²"Speak to Zerubbabel son of Shealtiel, governor of Judah, to Joshua son of Jehozadak, the high priest, and to the remnant of the people. Ask them, ³'Who of you is left who saw this house in its former glory? How does it look to you now? Does it not seem to you like nothing? ⁴But now be strong, O Zerubbabel,' declares the Lord. 'Be strong, O Joshua son of Jehozadak, the high priest. Be strong, all you people of the land,' declares the Lord, 'and work. For I am with you,' declares the Lord Almighty. ⁵'This is what I covenanted with you when you came out of Egypt. And my Spirit remains among you. Do not fear.'

At the beginning of this second word from the Lord, the cast is the same: the governor, the priest, and the people. The Lord asks these people, "Who of you is left who saw this house in its former glory? How does it look to you now? Does it not seem to you like nothing?"

These were questions the Lord wanted taken literally. Some in the crowd had seen the old temple. It had been destroyed 50 years earlier.

God calls our attention to the past. He even asks us, "Doesn't what exists today seem like nothing compared with what was?" Yet our God is not a God of the past, a "has-been" God. He works with us today. He is a God of the present. We are to be thinking of the present too. There is no dark age in the church. There is no golden age. There is, instead, the ever-ongoing present age of the church in which God's people, moved by his Spirit, do what he wills and pleases.

To be sure, there was the example in the past of the temple. But this does not mean that the believers of today are incapable of such a monument of love to their God, something just as good to give testimony to our faith. We don't look back like Lot's wife and turn to salt. We don't exist in the church for "the good old days." Today is the only day. The book of Hebrews says, "Today I have become your Father" (1:5). In Hebrews chapter 3 in discussing God's house, a number of times the Lord mentions "today." "Encourage one another daily, as long as it is called Today, so that none of you may be hardened by sin's deceitfulness" (verse 13).

In the face of the discouragement, the grandeur of the past, and the edifices that were, God speaks: "But now be strong and work . . . Do not fear."

There are three imperatives: be strong, work, and do not fear. Strength is required to overcome the inertia of sinful flesh, which is going to drag its feet when it comes to building God's house. Fear can cripple and hamstring the effort. The Lord says, "I am with you . . . Do not fear." With fear aside and strength at work, progress is made. In physics, work is defined as "the product of a force acting and the distance through which the force acts, the force and the distance being in the same direction." The Lord has worked it into his equation too.

The Lord is aware of the listless state we are in when it comes to building his house. The size of the work frightens us. We say lamely with the apostle Paul, "I have the desire to do what is good, but I cannot carry it out" (Romans 7:18). Into this void and empty state with its surrounding weakness and hesitancy, God sends his Spirit, who talks to our spirits and stirs them up: "Be strong and work and do not fear."

The Spirit speaks creative words. These are words with power and force in them, like the words "Let there be light." And there was light! Darkness retreated when God said those words. Fear and weakness must also retreat at the powerful words "Be strong and do not fear!"

This isn't a godly pep talk in which he tells us that we can do it if we look far enough inside ourselves. He isn't hinting at the fact that there may be latent reserves of power inside that we haven't tapped yet. No, the power comes from God. The courage comes from him. It comes through his words. We hear them, and what the words say happens. The proof of this is in the wonderful phrase "For I am with you."

> Fear not, I am with you. Oh, be not dismayed,
> For I am your God and will still give you aid;
> I'll strengthen you, help you,
>   and cause you to stand,
> Upheld by my righteous, omnipotent hand.
> (*Christian Worship* [CW] 416:3)

God's Spirit remains closely connected to the work at hand: "My Spirit remains among you. Do not fear." We think of Pentecost. Three thousand living stones were added to the church that day. No small work!

This work of getting people converted—building God's house—is the most challenging work. The believer is tempted to say, "They won't believe . . . they won't accept what I am saying . . . they won't support the work that we are trying to do for the Lord." We need to hear, "Be strong and work . . . my Spirit remains among you."

⁶"This is what the LORD Almighty says: 'In a little while I will once more shake the heavens and the earth, the sea and the dry land. ⁷I will shake all nations, and the desired of all nations will come, and I will fill this house with glory,' says the LORD Almighty. ⁸'The silver is mine and the gold is mine,' declares the LORD Almighty. ⁹'The glory of this present house will be greater than the glory of the former house,' says the LORD Almighty. 'And in this place I will grant peace,' declares the LORD Almighty."

This is now the seventh time the Lord addresses himself as "the LORD Almighty." The word *almighty* in the Hebrew language is the word for "hosts." It is used for the mass of fighting men that advances to do battle with the enemy. Remember that God is speaking through Haggai to a group, a remnant, of people. They very much felt the insecurity of life. They were outnumbered. In the face of this disadvantage they were also told to fight and build and accomplish things for their God. So the Lord wants them to know, "I am the God of hosts."

The prophet Elisha's servant was terrified one morning when he got up and saw Aramean enemy soldiers completely encircling their little village. "Oh, my lord, what shall we do?" the servant whispered hoarsely (2 Kings 6:15). "Don't be afraid," the prophet spoke calmly. "Those who are with us are more than those who are with them" (verse 16). And we read, "Then the LORD opened the servant's eyes, and he looked and saw the hills full of horses and chariots of fire all around Elisha" (verse 17). This is the Lord of hosts! These are his angels with their chariots of fire!

The Lord Almighty is not only a stirrer of spirits. He is also a shaker of nations. He says this in verse 7.

The prophecy of this great shaking is hard to pinpoint. Is it one time or is it speaking about a number of different shakings? One thing we determine with no questions—the coming of the desire (the darling) of the nations was the greatest upheaval in history. What happened in Bethlehem that Christmas night long ago is still sending its shock waves among the nations. The Savior came to the nations.

The word here for *nations* is the word *goyim*. This is often used by present-day Jews to refer to the Gentiles. The nations look to the coming Savior as the thirsty look into the desert's mirages and see a real oasis or as those lost in the night strain their eyes and see the welcome flickering of a fire.

They *desire* him. The meaning of the word *desire* is first that which answers longing and need. But the second meaning also includes the idea of a sweetheart or a loved one. The picture is beautiful and striking. The separated lovers see each other at a distance and run to meet each other. Is there any deeper excitement and joy known to human beings?

"Unless the LORD builds the house, its builders labor in vain. Unless the LORD watches over the city, the watchmen stand guard in vain" (Psalm 127:1). And, as the Lord points out in verse 7, unless he fills the house with his glory, it remains just a house, no matter how grand it may seem, no matter how costly it may be. (He reminds us, "The silver is mine and the gold is mine.") The glory of the church is not the magnificence of the edifice. The glory of the church is that simple people gather in something they have made with their hands at the stirring of the Spirit in them, and then God himself comes and lives with them! And this is his delight!

Verse 9 encourages us to know that the best Christians haven't all died. Greatness of religion is not just a thing of the past. The church at its best was not just the church of martyrs in arenas. It wasn't just the church of the Reformation with cathedrals echoing the words "Here I stand." We have God's promise that even today our humble efforts will produce something worthwhile, something inspiring, something that will give God the glory. The church does not sit back on its laurels. It constantly looks to the future, to the better, to more, to the greater. And if it should achieve the epitome of glory in this world, there still will remain the far transcending glory when the church militant becomes the church triumphant, and we all step from this world into the bright light of the world to come.

"'The glory of this present house will be greater than the glory of the former house,' says the LORD Almighty."

And peace! There will be peace, the peace that we crave. Peace of conscience. Peace in life. Peace among our people. Peace in our families. Peace in our world. Is it too much to expect? In this world, yes. The Lord tells us to prepare for wars and rumors of wars and for times getting worse. And yet, there is peace. There is peace that passes our human understanding. The pastor says these words every time he is finished with his sermon in church. It isn't peace that man can give. It isn't peace we can dissect and analyze. It is simply the peace of God, which he snows down on his people in quiet softness.

How many times the prophets and apostles spoke of this peace! And why? Because the people needed it so badly, because there was such a lack of peace. Jesus himself, in coming to his disciples, wishes them peace. To these fearful, timid, and faltering, Jesus said, "Peace!" The world didn't change. The uproar and unrest didn't stop. But the disciples knew this peace. They stepped out into the world. And as they were being stoned to death, they looked heavenward, smiled, and "fell asleep." Peace!

Give us peace like this, Lord. Fill our churches and lives with this peace. Keep your promise to us: "And in this place I will grant peace."

PART THREE

The Third Word from the Lord
(2:10-19)

A word of concern and a promise

¹⁰On the twenty-fourth day of the ninth month, in the second year of Darius, the word of the LORD came to the prophet Haggai: ¹¹"This is what the LORD Almighty says: 'Ask the priests what the law says: ¹²If a person carries consecrated meat in the fold of his garment, and that fold touches some bread or stew, some wine, oil or other food, does it become consecrated?'"

The priests answered, "No."

¹³Then Haggai said, "If a person defiled by contact with a dead body touches one of these things, does it become defiled?"

"Yes," the priests replied, "it becomes defiled."

¹⁴Then Haggai said, "'So it is with this people and this nation in my sight,' declares the LORD. 'Whatever they do and whatever they offer there is defiled.

¹⁵"'Now give careful thought to this from this day on—consider how things were before one stone was laid on another in the LORD's temple. ¹⁶When anyone came to a heap of twenty measures, there were only ten. When anyone went to a wine vat to draw fifty measures, there were only twenty. ¹⁷I struck all the work of your hands with blight, mildew and hail, yet you did not turn to me,' declares the LORD. ¹⁸'From this day on, from this twenty-fourth day of the ninth month, give careful thought to the day when the foundation of the LORD's temple was laid. Give careful thought: ¹⁹Is there yet any seed left in the barn? Until now, the vine and the fig tree, the pomegranate and the olive tree have not borne fruit.

"'From this day on I will bless you.'"

This is the third word of the Lord. Once again the date is listed. It was the 24th day of the ninth month, in the second year of Darius.

The Greek philosopher Socrates was known for his use of questions to lead people to make statements of truth. He taught them in this way. The Lord uses this method here. He asks questions. He deals with something known and leads to the unknown or, if not unknown, at least not something that has been confessed.

The people knew the facts, but they were not in the habit of applying them to themselves or to their situation. In this, times haven't changed. God's Word sounds so good when applied to others, but we miss the point in our own lives. The Lord comes to us with his divine rhetoric. If we hear him out, we have to confess what is right. We have to confess that he is right.

"Ask the priests what the law says," the Lord challenges. The priests knew. They were able to answer the questions that follow here. The people knew the answers too.

The general principle established by the Lord's questioning and the priest's answering in verse 12 is that bad makes something good turn into something bad more easily than good makes something that is bad into something good. In other words, "a little yeast works through the whole batch of dough" (1 Corinthians 5:6). After the battle of Jericho (Joshua 6), it was not the people's rightness that made Aachan's sin right; it was instead Aachan's sin that polluted the whole camp of Israel (Joshua 7). A little badness quickly leads to big badness.

So here in our verse, because of the general attitude, because of a present evil and slackness in the people, the Lord says through Haggai, "So it is with this people and this nation in my sight. . . . Whatever they do and whatever they offer there is defiled." We can hear the Lord musing to himself, "These people draw near to me with their mouths but their hearts are far from me."

Verses 15 to 19 refer back to the results of not building God's house: lack, blight, mildew, hail.

Then sounds the bell tone of verse 18, "From this day on, from this twenty-fourth day of the ninth month, give careful thought to the day when the foundation of the LORD's temple was laid." Do it today! Do it on this particular calendar day! In a spiritual sense we can't put off until tomorrow what can be done today. The night comes when no one can work. As the saying goes, the road to hell is paved with good intentions.

Our God wants us to ask ourselves this question: "What are we doing to ourselves?" Look at the results of lukewarm religion. Nothing is right. "Until now, the vine and the fig tree, the pomegranate and the olive tree have not borne fruit." Until now! But it isn't going to stay this way.

God is working among us. His Spirit is stirring hearts. Things are going to change. This is the eternal, godly optimism that the Word of God works as the law and gospel have their way in people's hearts and lives. We aren't doomed to failure. We aren't doomed to never being able to change. The Christian life is one of change. People get better; they are converted. They are reborn. They have a new spirit and new life instilled in their hearts.

Just as our God wants change to take place in our lives on "this day," so also he wants the blessings to start in our lives on "this day." The section ends with those beautiful words, "From this day on I will bless you."

PART FOUR

The Fourth Word from the Lord
(2:20-23)

A word of comfort to the ruler

²⁰The word of the LORD came to Haggai a second time on the twenty-fourth day of the month: ²¹"Tell Zerubbabel governor of Judah that I will shake the heavens and the earth. ²²I will overturn royal thrones and shatter the power of the foreign kingdoms. I will overthrow chariots and their drivers; horses and their riders will fall, each by the sword of his brother.

²³"'On that day,' declares the LORD Almighty, 'I will take you, my servant Zerubbabel son of Shealtiel,' declares the LORD, 'and I will make you like my signet ring, for I have chosen you,' declares the LORD Almighty."

The fourth and last word of the Lord in the book of Haggai starts at verse 20. This word is directed to the governor and the leader of the people, Zerubbabel. The word is a word that all rulers would love to hear. Their enemies are all going to be defeated. The previous section ended with God's stated will to bless. The ruler is included in this blessing. And certainly, if the earthly ruler is blessed, the people under him will be blessed too.

The people and ruler are to know that the phrase "In God we trust" is worth more than a stamp on our money. We want it emblazoned in our lives. When the ruler and his people trust in God, their nation is invincible. It is so because their God is invincible, and he goes on record: "I will overturn royal thrones and shatter the power of the foreign kingdoms. I will overthrow chariots and their drivers; horses and their riders will fall, each by the sword of his brother."

"If God is for us, who can be against us?" (Romans 8:31) is a question that holds true for the nation. The inverse is also true. If God is not for us, nothing can save us. Israel is a prime example of this fact. After Solomon's son Rehoboam took over the rule of Israel, there was not one godly ruler. One possible exception would be Jehu, who at the time of Ahab and Jezebel did clean house, but even about him we read, "Yet Jehu was not careful to keep the law of the LORD, the God of Israel" (2 Kings 10:31). For about two hundred years the kingdom of Israel suffered under these evil rulers until, with one last sigh, it entered oblivion in 722 B.C. In 2 Kings 17:8 we read about the last act of the scenario of the nation without God: "The LORD was very angry with Israel and removed them from his presence."

But Judah was different. Zerubbabel saw his people returned from captivity. He heard the Lord's blessing on him. He heard the promise. He was to be the Lord's signet ring.

In Genesis chapter 38 we read the sordid story of Judah and his illicit sexual relations with his daughter-in-law, Tamar. In that affair, Tamar asked Judah for some pledge of surety that he would send the young goat from his flock as he had promised. Judah gave as surety his seal, with its cord, and the staff in his hand" (verse 18). The seal was something that could identify him. It was his identification card.

The seal also had a part in the regalia of the priests and their clothing as the Lord prescribed it in the book of Exodus. In these signets, the names were in some way fashioned to be part of the seal. A king was known by his writing on his signet ring or scroll. It was by this that his authority was established. Throughout the Middle East, an embossed cylinder was rolled through soft wax to leave the impression of royalty and power for the beholder to witness.

Zerubbabel had God's name stamped across the face of his life. "I have chosen you," is what the Lord said. He was forever identified. He also stood to represent God's power. In view of the sweeping promises God had just made to him, he could say with the apostle Paul, "If God is for me, who can be against me?"

In Revelation chapter 7 the angel coming up from the east called out in a loud voice to the angels who had been given power to harm the land and the sea: "Do not harm the land or the sea or the trees until we put a seal on the foreheads of the servants of our God" (verse 3).

God's children have his mark upon them; they in turn put their mark (his mark) on the world. We carry with us the name Jesus. We are the people that name represents when it claims to be Savior. We are the proof of his name and of his claim.

Some may notice that the events described to Zerubbabel in promise never happened in his lifetime. There wasn't a time when the royal thrones were overthrown and the powers were shattered. The kings of the Persian Empire continued to succeed in relatively peaceful fashion.

The reference to Zerubbabel in the book of Haggai is not to a specific person but to the position or the throne of ruling. Zerubbabel is listed in both genealogies of Jesus in the New Testament (Matthew 1; Luke 3). He is one ruler in the line of the Ruler, the one to whom every knee will bow and every tongue will confess. In Luke 1:32,33 the angel said to troubled Mary: "He [Jesus] will be great and will be called the Son of the Most High. The Lord God will give him the throne of his father David, and he will reign over the house of Jacob forever; his kingdom will never end."

The greatest of all battles the Savior fought was the one on Golgotha; it was there that he forever shattered the power of the "foreign kingdoms." This happened and was proven by Jesus' words, "It is finished" (John 19:30). The enmity between God and man was over, the enmity that hailed back to the beginning, the snake, and the two wretched transgressors.

Jesus said his kingdom was not of this world. We should not insist on finding literal representation of Haggai's prophecy in the lives of the kings of this world. The Lord God came and did real battle with the spiritual forces of evil. He overthrew them completely, and he won. The prophecy was completed and fulfilled.

Any believer, Zerubbabel included, realizes that his greatest dangers and threat do not come from the quarters of this world's military groups. Rather, our greatest struggles are "against the rulers, against the authorities, against the powers of this dark world and against the spiritual forces of evil in the heavenly realms" (Ephesians 6:12). These words of prophecy are fulfilled every time God's children win the fight as John describes it: "You, dear children, are from God and have overcome them, because the one who is in you is greater than the one who is in the world" (1 John 4:4).

With his certain statement of having chosen Zerubbabel and with the word *almighty* ringing in our ears, the Lord closes this small but important book.

INTRODUCTION TO ZECHARIAH

Historical background

Zechariah was a contemporary of Haggai. He too had seen the captivity and had returned. With Haggai, he saw the people's apathy toward building God's house. He joined in the message of Haggai, who spoke for God: "Build my house!"

The book begins with the first word of the Lord to Zechariah, coming just two months after Haggai's first word, in the eighth month of the second year of Darius, in 520 B.C. (For a discussion of the reigns of the various Persian kings, see page 1.)

The book of Ezra tells us, "Haggai the prophet and Zechariah the prophet, a descendant of Iddo, prophesied to the Jews in Judah and Jerusalem in the name of the God of Israel, who was over them" (5:1).

Zerubbabel and Jeshua were at work rebuilding the house of God in Jerusalem. Ezra further tells us: "The elders of the Jews continued to build and prosper under the preaching of Haggai the prophet and Zechariah, a descendant of Iddo. They finished building the temple according to the command of the God of Israel and the decrees of Cyrus, Darius and Artaxerxes" (6:14).

There are many striking pictures in the book of Zechariah. Some of them are surrealistic and in kaleidoscopic colors. Some are stark and strange. Zechariah painted with a prophetic brush on the imaginations and consciences of his people. We come upon these paintings today and see that over the years the colors have not faded and the images have not been blurred. He painted hell and heaven; he preached God's law and gospel.

Zechariah was also a prophet who spoke words directly describing the coming Savior. In this book we will hear words that we recognize from the passion history of our Lord. Zechariah knew the Savior by inspiration and prophecy.

Outline

I. The first word (1:1–6:15)
    A. The return (1:1-6)
    B. The visions (1:7–6:8)
    C. The Branch (6:9-15)

II. The second word (7:1–8:23)
    A. Religion, but not to God (7:1-7)
    B. Hard hearts (7:8-14)
    C. The Lord promises good (8:1-23)

III. The prophecies of the messianic King (9:1–14:21)
    A. The kings will be destroyed (9:1-8)
    B. The King will come (9:9-17)
    C. The curse on the shepherds (10:1–11:3)
    D. The Shepherd and his two staffs (11:4-17)
    E. Strength (12:1-9)
    F. Mourning (12:10-14)
    G. The Shepherd struck, the sheep scattered (13:1-9)
    H. The Lord comes (14:1-21)

PART ONE

The First Word
(1:1–6:15)

A call to return to the Lord

1 In the eighth month of the second year of Darius, the word of the LORD came to the prophet Zechariah son of Berekiah, the son of Iddo:

²"The LORD was very angry with your forefathers. ³Therefore tell the people: This is what the LORD Almighty says: 'Return to me,' declares the LORD Almighty, 'and I will return to you,' says the LORD Almighty. ⁴Do not be like your forefathers, to whom the earlier prophets proclaimed: This is what the LORD Almighty says: 'Turn from your evil ways and your evil practices.' But they would not listen or pay attention to me, declares the LORD. ⁵Where are your forefathers now? And the prophets, do they live forever? ⁶But did not my words and my decrees, which I commanded my servants the prophets, overtake your forefathers?"

"Then they repented and said, 'The LORD Almighty has done to us what our ways and practices deserve, just as he determined to do.'"

The prophet's name is Zechariah. The name means either "Yahweh remembers" or "the one remembered by Yahweh." The Jews were people who, like the American Indians, had names that meant something. Our names today mean something too, but because they come at birth, before a personality develops or deeds are done, they don't have the significance they used to have. Who knows, for instance, that the name Philip means "lover of horses"?

In the name Zechariah we have a testimony that someone had the belief that our God, Yahweh, remembers. What a good name it is! What a great aid to go through life with a name that reminds the bearer that his God remembers him and remembers all of the promises connected to him by grace. Certainly the name would stand the prophet in good stead.

Zechariah was the son of Berekiah, who was the son of Iddo. He was a human being. He had a father, and his father in turn had a father. They were subjected to all of the experiences of human life, both positive and negative. When the Savior of the world would come, he too would have a family tree. The Bible calls special attention to Jesus' parentage. Twice it is listed (Matthew 1:1; Luke 3:23); the first is his legal lineage through Joseph, and the second, his bloodline through Mary.

As we begin the study of Zechariah, the topic of fathers is important. The words begin, "The LORD was very angry with your forefathers." Fathers not only help to determine their children's physical characteristics, but they also influence their spiritual characteristics.

The sins of fathers come down to their children. What our fathers are and were is a concern to us. The Lord points that out in these first verses. His encouragement is, "Do not be like your forefathers." "The LORD was very angry with your forefathers." This is a side of God most people would rather not see. Christians even receive stares of indignation if they dare to tell someone that God is a God who gets angry, so angry that he blows the fires of hell hotter. People who do not know God and who do not want to know him are quick to suppose and defend the idea that God can only be a kind, old grandfatherly type who smiles down in benevolence upon children who, though sometimes rowdy and naughty, are for the most part "nice kids."

Zechariah told his people about the angry God. The Hebrew here would be literally translated, "The LORD burned with an angry anger." The KJV reads Psalm 7:11 to say, "God is angry *with the wicked* every day." The Lord is not vindictive, nor is he, as some say, after his "shylockian pound of flesh." Rather, he is a just God who cannot tolerate evil. In his righteousness he cannot stand that a single infraction be unpunished. If he could, he would not be truly and completely holy. If he could look the other way in self-deception or in hopeless inability, then he would not be the righteous and almighty God he claims to be.

God has no pleasure when the wicked perish. "Return to me," he says. That is another way of saying, "Be converted! Repent! Turn from your evil ways and your evil practices." The Lord wants people to change their minds about him. In the context of the book of Zechariah, he is also saying: "Change your minds about what is important in life. Look at my house in ruins. Get your priorities straight. Seek first the kingdom of God and his righteousness, and all these things will be added to you. As your fathers are examples of the wrath that comes on those I hate because of their sin, so also are they examples of the love that I show to those who turn from their sin. How often didn't they call to me in their trouble, and I delivered them? All I wanted them to do was to turn to me and call on my name. They left me; I did not leave them. When they returned to me, I returned to them."

When the Lord said, "Return to me, and I will return to you," he did not mean that people have the ability to make the first move back to God on their own and then, after God sees the effort on their parts, he comes to them. The Word makes it clear that it is God who works in us to will

37

and to do of his good pleasure. The examples are count-less of the Lord working it so that his children return, sending pestilence, enemies, and trouble and then remind-ing them of a God who has mercy and love. The book of Haggai tells us, "I struck all the work of your hands with blight, mildew and hail, yet you did not turn to me" (2:17).

Still, in it all, the Lord does appeal to us to turn. It is not he who turns. He tells us to turn. His people *do* turn to him. They call on his name. They ask for forgiveness in his name and he grants it. They say with David, "Cre-ate in me a pure heart, O God, and renew a steadfast spirit within me" (Psalm 51:10). Like David, we desire to change our ways of thinking and doing things. We want to turn and return.

The consequences of not returning are awful. "Where are your forefathers now?" the Lord questions in verse 5.

Somehow the children must rise above the examples of their fathers. How difficult this is to do! The Lord points out, "Fathers . . . bring [your children] up in the training and instruction of the Lord" (Ephesians 6:4). "Train a child in the way he should go, and when he is old he will not turn from it" (Proverbs 22:6). But what do children do when their fathers do not do what is right? It must be the Lord who somehow comes to the children and says, "Do not be like your forefathers." It must be the Lord who makes it possible for children to break loose from the stranglehold their fathers' examples have on them.

This happens. We see it in the lives of those dear people who live godly and faithful lives in spite of the terrible examples they had at home. We wonder, "Why do they do it? Why do they come to church?" The answer must lie in these verses. The Lord has impressed upon them the neces-sity of being better than their fathers.

Prophets do not live forever. The warning to return is not going to be voiced indefinitely. It was written at the time of Samuel (a thousand years before the Savior was born): "In those days the word of the LORD was rare; there were not many visions" (1 Samuel 3:1). God had taken his Word away from people who didn't want to hear it.

Implicit in Zechariah's words is that if the warning is not heeded, there will come a time when the Lord will no longer ask us to turn. Finally Moses did not return to Pharaoh—and the silence was deafening.

What a spellbinding drama it is in verse 6 as the people strayed closer and closer to the edge of disaster, and the Word pursued them persistently. Will the brand be snatched from the fire before it is consumed? Will the smoking wick and the bruised reed be somehow kept from ruination?

God's law and gospel bound out after straying sinners: "Repent! Return!" We read, "Then they repented and said, 'The LORD Almighty has done to us what our ways and practices deserve, just as he determined to do.'"

God is just. Even those who do not believe in him will ultimately have to admit his justice. "We are punished justly, for we are getting what our deeds deserve," the thief on the cross next to Jesus confessed (Luke 23:41). God is also just in forgiving. His Son has paid the price. To those who claim the Son as a sacrifice for their sins, God will do just as he determined to do; he will forgive them! He will receive them into his kingdom of grace and power. Just as he determines to damn the stubborn sinner, so he also determines to save the sorry saint.

The man among the myrtle trees

⁷On the twenty-fourth day of the eleventh month, the month of Shebat, in the second year of Darius, the word of the LORD came to the prophet Zechariah son of Berekiah, the son of Iddo.

39

⁸During the night I had a vision—and there before me was a man riding a red horse! He was standing among the myrtle trees in a ravine. Behind him were red, brown and white horses.

⁹I asked, "What are these, my lord?"

The angel who was talking with me answered, "I will show you what they are."

¹⁰Then the man standing among the myrtle trees explained, "They are the ones the LORD has sent to go throughout the earth."

¹¹And they reported to the angel of the LORD, who was standing among the myrtle trees, "We have gone throughout the earth and found the whole world at rest and in peace."

¹²Then the angel of the LORD said, "LORD Almighty, how long will you withhold mercy from Jerusalem and from the towns of Judah, which you have been angry with these seventy years?" ¹³So the LORD spoke kind and comforting words to the angel who talked with me.

¹⁴Then the angel who was speaking to me said, "Proclaim this word: This is what the LORD Almighty says: 'I am very jealous for Jerusalem and Zion, ¹⁵but I am very angry with the nations that feel secure. I was only a little angry, but they added to the calamity.'

¹⁶"Therefore, this is what the LORD says: 'I will return to Jerusalem with mercy, and there my house will be rebuilt. And the measuring line will be stretched out over Jerusalem,' declares the LORD Almighty.

¹⁷"Proclaim further: This is what the LORD Almighty says: 'My towns will again overflow with prosperity, and the LORD will again comfort Zion and choose Jerusalem.'"

Verse 7 puts the following visions into a time context. They occurred about three months after the first word of the Lord had come to Zechariah. That was exactly five months after the building of the temple had been resumed (Haggai 1:15).

There is some difficulty with the colors of the horses. First, we are tempted to speculate as to what the colors mean. When all is said and done, we have to admit that we do not know what the colors signify. Second, there is some question as to what should be translated "brown" and what should be translated "red." The word translated "red" is related to the names Adam and Edom (Esau). Neither Adam, taken from the ground, nor Esau, who was ruddy in complexion, were bright red in color. The word is spelled the same way in Hebrew as the word for *ground*. This would give us the idea that it would be closer to brown than to red. But then the dictionary also lists as meanings "the color of grape juice" and "blood."

But let us not get bogged down in trying to figure out the color and its meaning. Can we just notice that to Zechariah's mind and eye, the horses were of different colors? This was a dream! A vision! They had colors Zechariah could identify.

As to the question of what the horses are, Zechariah asked this question himself in verse 9, and he receives an answer in verses 10 and following.

The horses were beings sent by God himself to go throughout the earth. Angels are pictured as horses in other places. Elisha comforted his frightened servant, who saw the enemy surrounding them: "'Don't be afraid,' the prophet answered. 'Those who are with us are more than those who are with them.' And Elisha prayed, 'O LORD, open his eyes so he may see.' Then the LORD opened the servant's eyes, and he looked and saw the hills full of horses and chariots of fire all around Elisha" (2 Kings 6:16,17). At the time when Elijah was taken up to heaven, we hear, "Suddenly a chariot of fire and horses of fire appeared and separated the two of them" (2 Kings 2:11). If we compare this trip to heaven with the trip the angels made with the beggar Lazarus (Luke 16:22), then we can make a connection between horses and angels. We remember, of course, that in their natural state, angels are invisible because they are spiritual beings.

The angels had done their work well. They had gone "throughout" the earth. The word here is the one that means to walk to and fro. It is the same word that the devil said when asked where he had been in Job's life: "Roaming through the earth and *going back and forth* in it" (Job 1:7).

The devil is roaming to and fro. It is comforting to know that the angels of God also roam to and fro. They have a special mission of search and rescue (see Psalm 91). They are special forces—crack forces—appointed by God for the safety and welfare of his people.

The angels in Zechariah's vision reported that there was universal peace and rest. But there was one flaw. The angel of the Lord himself pointed it out: "LORD Almighty, how long will you withhold mercy from Jerusalem and from the towns of Judah, which you have been angry with these seventy years?" It does not seem fair. The heathen had rest and peace. God's people had just come out of 70 years' worth of persecution and affliction. Would there be retribution? Would the course of events be justified and things put on their right course again?

The Lord Almighty himself answered: "I am very jealous for Jerusalem and Zion, but I am very angry with the nations that feel secure. I was only a little angry, but they added to the calamity."

The Lord Almighty jealous? Of what? Of children who went astray, did evil, and turned their backs on their Father? Yes, he was jealous for these reasons. As great as his love is, so great is his jealousy. His First Commandment stems from this burning jealousy: "Have no other gods before me" (Exodus 20:3). We understand, in our imperfect way, what the Lord feels. No one who has a sweetheart wants to be second on the list. No one who loves another feels good when he or she sees that "beloved" giving love and affection to another.

In his righteous, perfect way, the Lord is jealous for his people. Because he is jealous and because he does not give up on them easily, he does everything in his power to bring them back to their senses and to him. Seventy years of captivity in this case was the effort of the Lord not only to cause his people to long for the land he had given to their forefathers, but to long for him and his house.

The nations felt secure, but God was very angry with them. It seems they enjoyed peace and quiet, prosperity and riches. But appearances can be deceiving. Asaph, the writer of Psalm 73, wrestled with this seeming discrepancy when he wrote: "I envied the arrogant when I saw the prosperity of the wicked. They have no struggles; their bodies are healthy and strong. They are free from the burdens common to man; they are not plagued by human ills" (verses 3-5). But then Asaph came to this realization: "How suddenly are they destroyed, completely swept away by terrors!" (verse 19). The weeds are allowed to grow unmolested with the wheat for a while, but the day comes when they will be gathered and thrown into the fire.

But there are kind, comforting words for God's people: "So the LORD spoke kind and comforting words to the angel who talked with me." Part of these words of comfort seems to be the skewering of the wicked by the words, "I was only a little angry, but they added to the calamity."

The implication is that the wicked went beyond their bounds as God's method for correcting his people. They supported the evil. They added to it. And although God did use earthly means to chastise his people, listen to what Isaiah the prophet says: "O my people who live in Zion, do not be afraid of the Assyrians, who beat you with a rod and lift up a club against you, as Egypt did. Very soon my anger against you will end and my wrath will be directed to their destruction. The Lord Almighty will lash them with a whip" (10:24-26). In other words, God makes a whip to chastise his people, and then he whips the whip!

The words are comforting. They speak further of help and aid from the God who may be angry with his people. In the New Testament times, we live with the promise of the Comforter. This is God's Holy Spirit, who wants to continue in the pattern of the past by speaking kind and comforting words to his people.

God's house will be rebuilt. It will be rebuilt according to the straightness of the string. Each block will be laid exactly and true. The church will be built to stand according to divine specifications: "In him the whole building is joined together and rises to become a holy temple in the Lord" (Ephesians 2:21).

Our section closes in verse 17 with a twofold promise: comfort and choosing.

The mother comforts her child because she wants to. It comes from within her. The Hebrew word for *mercy,* of which we have heard several times in these verses, is a word that also means "the womb." This is where the people who heard Zechariah's message considered mercy coming from. The mother cannot help herself. When she sees the fruit of her womb in trouble, discouraged, and hurting, her mother's heart and feelings yearn to comfort that child. So it is with God.

The Lord "chose" Jerusalem. Any child on the playground knows the thrill in this word. When the children are mustered out to play, the captains step forward to pick "theirs." The little boy watches his hero, and the hero's eyes meet the little boy's. His name is called! His heart beats quickly! He steps proudly over to be on the team of the one he admires. Many children also know the pain of standing and waiting and waiting to be chosen while other names are called.

Imagine, then, the Lord looking at each of us and saying, "I want *you* on my side!" "Lord, 'tis not that I did choose you; that, I know, could never be." Then we sing, "It was grace in Christ that called me" (CW 380:2). The Lord chose Jerusalem.

Four horns and four craftsmen

¹⁸Then I looked up—and there before me were four horns! ¹⁹I asked the angel who was speaking to me, "What are these?"

He answered me, "These are the horns that scattered Judah, Israel and Jerusalem."

²⁰Then the LORD showed me four craftsmen. ²¹I asked, "What are these coming to do?"

He answered, "These are the horns that scattered Judah so that no one could raise his head, but the craftsmen have come to terrify them and throw down these horns of the nations who lifted up their horns against the land of Judah to scatter its people."

A man with a measuring line

2 Then I looked up—and there before me was a man with a measuring line in his hand! ²I asked, "Where are you going?"

He answered me, "To measure Jerusalem, to find out how wide and how long it is."

³Then the angel who was speaking to me left, and another angel came to meet him ⁴and said to him: "Run, tell that young man, 'Jerusalem will be a city without walls because of the great number of men and livestock in it. ⁵And I myself will be a wall of fire around it,' declares the LORD, 'and I will be its glory within.'

Destruction comes with four horns. Deliverance comes through four craftsmen.

This little prophecy gives us a commentary on the work of the devil and on the work of God. The one is bent on destruction and ruin. The other is determined to save and reconstruct. Basically, the devil tries to destroy and root up. He uses the horn, the symbol of power, to accomplish this.

It is with the horn that the bull causes all of the damage his mighty body is capable of. All of his strength is focused on that one point as he charges angrily at his cowering victim. Here the horn is the symbol of the devil's power. "Our struggle is not against flesh and blood, but against the rulers, against the authorities, against the powers of this dark world and against the spiritual forces of evil" (Ephesians 6:12).

The Lord, on the other hand, is a craftsman of singular accomplishment. He takes what is ruined, bent, and spoiled and repairs, restores, and redeems it. When there was no hope, when "no one could raise his head," he came and worked in his mighty way. Then, in turn, the great Craftsman, who summons his craftsmen, is going to place the powers of evil in a place of terror and destruction. The Craftsman is finally going to destroy. Hell is real, and hell is not remedial. Hell is the place of terror reserved for all the nations who used power to scatter God's people.

The third frame of the vision of Zechariah comes in chapter 2.

Zechariah recognized a man. He also recognized a measuring line. He did not ask "Who?" He did recognize the need to ask "Where?" Perhaps the mien and manner of the man prompted the question. The man seemed anxious to do the work that the measuring string in his hand promised he would do.

The answer to Zechariah's question "Where are you going?" is, "To measure Jerusalem." The further reason for knowing these dimensions is the construction of the wall of fire around it, for it is to be a city not protected by earthly ramparts but surrounded by God's power and might.

We are reminded of the glory cloud, the visible sign of God's protecting presence as the Israelites fled from Pharaoh—a fire by night and a cloud by day. They didn't need further armament or protection. It was enough.

When God is the protection of his people Jerusalem, of his believers, there is no fear or failure, no surprise attack or storm that breaches the walls. "Unless the LORD watches over the city, the watchmen stand guard in vain" (Psalm 127:1).

This Jerusalem surrounded by the wall of fire is the same Jerusalem that the book of Revelation talks about in chapters 21 and 22. "The city does not need the sun or the moon to shine on it, for the glory of God gives it light, and the Lamb is its lamp. The nations will walk by its light, and the kings of the earth will bring their splendor into it. On no day will its gates ever be shut, for there will be no night there. The glory and honor of the nations will be brought into it" (21:23-26).

The walls of ancient cities were the life insurance of the people inside. The gates were closed at night to keep out enemies. If the walls failed, the people died. If the walls held, the people lived. Many ancient stories deal with the walls. We have the Trojan horse in Greek mythology. Cyrus was alleged to have diverted the river so his troops could march through the water gates into the city of Babylon.

Both Zechariah and the apostle John saw the Lord as the glory of the Holy City. They saw the city standing secure without a wall of human construction. And they saw it filled to overflowing. Here is the second reason why the new Jerusalem will be a city without walls. Walls would not hold the burgeoning population inside, "because of the great number of men and livestock in it." John spoke also: "Nothing impure will ever enter it, nor will anyone who does what is shameful or deceitful, but only those whose names are written in the Lamb's book of life" (Revelation 21:27). All God's people will enter it!

⁶"Come! Come! Flee from the land of the north," declares the Lᴏʀᴅ, "for I have scattered you to the four winds of heaven," declares the Lᴏʀᴅ.
⁷"Come, O Zion! Escape, you who live in the Daughter of Babylon!" ⁸For this is what the Lᴏʀᴅ Almighty says: "After he has honored me and has sent me against the nations that have plundered you—for whoever touches you touches the apple of his eye—⁹I will surely raise my hand against them so that their slaves will plunder them. Then you will know that the Lᴏʀᴅ Almighty has sent me.
¹⁰"Shout and be glad, O Daughter of Zion. For I am coming, and I will live among you," declares the Lᴏʀᴅ. ¹¹"Many nations will be joined with the Lᴏʀᴅ in that day and will become my people. I will live among you and you will know that the Lᴏʀᴅ Almighty has sent me to you. ¹²The Lᴏʀᴅ will inherit Judah as his portion in the holy land and will again choose Jerusalem. ¹³Be still before the Lᴏʀᴅ, all mankind, because he has roused himself from his holy dwelling."

Some translations of verse 6 read "Ho! Ho!" instead of "Come! Come!" The word in Hebrew is the word that is still used in the Yiddish expression *Hoi! Weh!* It can mean "Woe!" In fact, the two sound the same. It is a word spoken under great urgency to get someone's attention.

We can see the Lord beckoning. We can hear him saying, "Ho! Ho!" or "Come! Come!" Get away from the destruction that is coming from the north, from Babylon (it is referred to in this way in other places; see Jeremiah 1:14; 6:22).

Once again, the land that punished God's people was in turn going to receive punishment: "I will surely raise my hand against them so that their slaves will plunder them."

Six centuries before Christ, Babylon was the whip God used to chastise his people. But Babylon's time for punishment came. Their slaves plundered them.

God's people remained the apple of his eye. Notice that in verse 8 this remark is a parenthetical remark made by the angel. The angel, who is by his commission a ministering spirit to God's people, knew the special and unique position of God's people. They were like the pupil, the gateway, to his eye. They were special to him. He saw them. No one could hurt them with impunity.

The theme of verses 10 to 13 is "I am coming to live with you." This is Immanuel—God with us. And if God is with us, who can be against us? Worry and anxiety come because we forget the fact that God is with us.

Our way home leads us past the bully's house. Down through the ages, God's people have feared the prospect, even to the point of not wanting to go home. But then they look up and see their Champion, and he says, "I am with you." Whether to Zechariah's people, a group of terrified disciples about to enter their ministry in this world, or to us in this modern day, the message is the same. Our need is the same. "Do not fear, for I am with you; do not be dismayed, for I am your God. I will strengthen you and help you; I will uphold you with my righteous right hand" (Isaiah 41:10).

Verse 11 promises that this God who wants to live with his people also wants to live among the nations. We have a special reason to be thankful for this, since most of us who read this book are Gentiles. God wants to live among us too. We are included in the Jewish religion led by the Jew Jesus. We cannot claim a genealogy in one of the 12 tribes, but we can claim a part in the inheritance of the kingdom to come.

Verse 13 begins with the translated words "Be still!" The Hebrew word is *Has!* In English we say the same thing when, with urgency, we say to someone who is making noise when they should not be, "Sssshhh!" "Sssshhh! Our God is here!"

There is another reason to be quiet: "He has roused himself from his holy dwelling." This too is a picture that Zechariah's people understood better than we do today.

This is the picture of a lion rising suddenly from his hidden liar and shaking himself. He looks around. Something has disturbed him, but there is no fear in his eyes. The hackles on his neck rise. Someone has challenged his holy place, and lions don't back down.

The Lion of Judah has risen from his hiding place. No one suspected that he was there. No one worried about his power and his presence—when they couldn't see him. But when he rises, they are rooted to the spot in fear. Even his own are awestruck. This is the one on our side! "Great Captain, now Thine arm make bare, Fight for us once again!" (*The Lutheran Hymnal* [TLH] 263:4).

"Be still before the LORD, *all* mankind!"

Clean clothes for a soiled servant

3 Then he showed me Joshua the high priest standing before the angel of the LORD, and Satan standing at his right side to accuse him. ²The LORD said to Satan, "The LORD rebuke you, Satan! The LORD, who has chosen Jerusalem, rebuke you! Is not this man a burning stick snatched from the fire?"

³Now Joshua was dressed in filthy clothes as he stood before the angel. ⁴The angel said to those who were standing before him, "Take off his filthy clothes."

Then he said to Joshua, "See, I have taken away your sin, and I will put rich garments on you."

⁵Then I said, "Put a clean turban on his head." So they put a clean turban on his head and clothed him, while the angel of the LORD stood by.

The main character of chapter 3 is Joshua, the high priest. Without saying that he typifies all priests, he is certainly a human being. And being a human being, the same thing afflicted him that afflicts all human beings: Satan accused him.

Being a priest or a minister does not make a person free from the charges that the devil levels. In fact, the charges intensify. If the devil doesn't hesitate to accuse the high priest, think of what he will do with the layperson. If he can point out the sin of the person who has been called to make religion his full-time occupation, then what can he do to the person who, at least so far as his life's work is concerned, has religion as a part-time occupation?

The ministerium needs to pay attention. Ministers need to remember that they are no better in God's sight or the devil's sight than the people they minister to. In the book of Hebrews, this is made very clear: "Every high priest is selected from among men and is appointed to represent them in matters related to God, to offer gifts and sacrifices for sins. He is able to deal gently with those who are ignorant and are going astray, since he himself is subject to weakness. This is why he has to offer sacrifices for his own sins, as well as for the sins of the people" (Hebrews 5:1-3).

In chapter 3 of the book of Zechariah, we see why Jesus, our High Priest, is so important to us. When he stepped before God for us, he did not do it with the devil's accusations ringing in his ears. His own Father was able to say, "This is my Son, whom I love; with him I am well pleased" (Matthew 17:5). The same writer of the book of Hebrews quoted above was able to write by inspiration, "We have one [high priest] who has been tempted in every way, just as we are—yet was without sin" (4:15).

The minister stands before his people. He is like Joshua, the priest. He prays for them on Sunday morning from the altar. He gives them the Lord's Supper and baptizes their children. He presents God's Word to them in preaching and in promise. If he is truly in the Word and about the Word, then he better than all others realizes the condemnation. The mirror of God's law is unmercifully clear as the minister peers into it. He knows the dream of the prophet Zechariah. He knows that Satan stands at his right side to accuse him. In this way and at this time, Satan is not a liar. The accusations are true! So the minister carries a double burden. If he is supposed to be the spiritual leader of his people, and Satan accuses him rightfully of so many transgressions, then what hope can there be for either him or his people?

This is Satan. He delights in accusing people before God. His very name means "adversary," "the one who carries a grudge." The word in Hebrew for *Satan* contains the very same letters as the verb *accuse*. It could be said, then, that "Satan was standing there at his right side to 'satan' him."

But then verse 2 comes! The great defense attorney rose. His words rung out loud and clear: "The Lord rebuke you, Satan! The Lord, who has chosen Jerusalem, rebuke you!" The cowering Joshua heard it, and he was glad. Never mind that he was compared to a burning stick snatched from the fire. It was true, and he knew it. But his Lord—the Lord, the Savior—had just defended him! His Lord had stepped before the accuser with his own name. He has authority over sin because he paid for sin. In God's court this Lord's words reign supreme. Their echo silenced the accuser.

This is the name proclaimed to Moses: "The Lord, the Lord, the compassionate and gracious God, slow to anger, abounding in love and faithfulness, maintaining love to thousands, and forgiving wickedness, rebellion and sin" (Exodus 34:6,7).

This Lord comes and chooses his people. He chooses to defend them against seemingly hopeless odds. This Lord snatches them from the fire. What a picture of our condition and God's action! He braved the fire to rescue his people. They were almost gone, yet he snatched them from the fire. That includes ministers no less than others.

Verses 3 to 5 carry on the beautiful imagery, words the accused of this world never tire of hearing. The very reason for the accusation was taken away. The dirty clothes, which in verse 4 are equated with sins, were taken away.

God does not get rid of the charge by ignoring the evil. Something had to be done with Joshua's dirty clothes. One thing was certain to all: Joshua could not stand before God wearing dirty clothes. The devil pointed to the smudges and stains. Joshua was painfully aware that he was standing before royalty with dirt as a covering. The Almighty and the Pure allows no dirt in his courtroom.

Yet it is all taken care of in a simple operation: "Take off his filthy clothes. I will put rich garments on you." When it was over, the accuser saw only spotlessly clean garments. Where was the charge now? Case dismissed. Everything was covered. The room was filled with rightness and righteousness. Joshua's heart and lips said, "Thank you, Lord," and his chest heaved a great sigh of relief. Now he could approach God and intercede for his fellow sinners. Now no one could accuse him. He was cleansed by the same soap that he recommended his hearers use on their dirty garments, their sins.

A hymn verse tells us how it is: "Clothed in his righteousness alone, faultless to stand before his throne." And why? "My hope is built on nothing less than Jesus' blood and righteousness" (CW 382:1,4). He is our clean clothes. He is the solid rock of trust and confidence upon which we stand.

The devil still pointed, but he was pointing at God's own Son, and even Satan realized the awful blasphemy of this, and he became very quiet.

A clean walk

⁶**The angel of the LORD gave this charge to Joshua:** ⁷**"This is what the LORD Almighty says: 'If you will walk in my ways and keep my requirements, then you will govern my house and have charge of my courts, and I will give you a place among these standing here.**

⁸**"'Listen, O high priest Joshua and your associates seated before you, who are men symbolic of things to come: I am going to bring my servant, the Branch.** ⁹**See, the stone I have set in front of Joshua! There are seven eyes on that one stone, and I will engrave an inscription on it,' says the LORD Almighty, 'and I will remove the sin of this land in a single day.**

¹⁰**"'In that day each of you will invite his neighbor to sit under his vine and fig tree,' declares the LORD Almighty."**

What takes place in verses 6 and 7 is really the same thing that happened to the woman taken in adultery in John chapter 8. The teachers of the law and Pharisees brought her to Jesus, and after all of the accusers had left after Jesus said, "If any one of you is without sin, let him be the first to throw a stone at her" (verse 7), Jesus told the woman, "Neither do I condemn you . . . Go now and leave your life of sin" (verse 11).

To Joshua the words were, "Walk in my ways and keep my requirements." This was the warning not to go back to the mud with his clean garments.

God's ministers are servants. They follow orders as servants, and orders are given here. If they are not walking the way and keeping the requirements, then they forfeit their positions as ministers. So their prayer as servants must be, "Lord, keep me faithful; keep me obedient."

What a shame when the minister fails and must step down from his position. It happens. Sad to say, it happens more and more as the ones in charge of God's courts are themselves unable to hear what he has to say about them and their families, their finances, and their future. The ministry gives no one a carte blanche. It is possible for a man to serve the Lord only as long as he walks in God's ways.

In the book of Hebrews, Jesus is called the High Priest. This is one of the themes of the book. As such he is the perfect "go-between" with God and man. He is the perfect revealer of God's will to man. He is also the perfect sacrifice.

Joshua and his friends were to be a preview of Jesus, the High Priest. Verse 8 says, "Listen, O high priest Joshua and your associates seated before you, who are men symbolic of things to come: I am going to bring my servant, the Branch." In this way the office of the priesthood was to be one way the Lord drew pictures in the minds of his people about the one who was coming to minister to all of their needs.

To us in the New Testament times, our ministers still go by the name of shepherd (pastor), realizing that there is one Shepherd, the Good Shepherd. The shepherds in churches, imperfect though they be, are symbolic of the Good Shepherd, the one who is coming to gather his sheep to his right hand.

Jesus is referred to with the words "the Branch." That this is he will become more evident in chapter 6 starting at verse 12. God makes certain abstract things about his Son clear with this picture of the branch.

In John chapter 15 Jesus himself uses this picture of the branch to picture the relationship of his people to himself. As the Branch, Jesus too is connected to his Father. He is his Father's Son. He did the will of his Father. He received his strength from his Father as a branch receives its strength from the root, the vine. We see this in many instances of Jesus praying to his Father, of angels coming to minister to him, of him withdrawing by himself to pray, and of him praying before meals.

In his life, Jesus was the very picture of a branch, a person who needed the constant care and supply his Father provided.

The purpose of the branch is to carry out the will of the root—to bear fruit. Jesus hinted at this when he referred to himself as the one who would "bringeth forth much fruit" (John 12:24 KJV). People looked at his life and said, "He has done everything well" (Mark 7:37). There would be much fruit in his life. John even said about him: "Jesus did many other things as well. If every one of them were written down, I suppose that even the whole world would not have room for the books that would be written" (John 21:25).

Jesus, the Branch, showed his disciples that he would not tolerate fruitlessness when he cursed the fig tree that had no fruit on it (Matthew 21:19). As the Branch, he knew what could reasonably be expected of branches.

Finally, in the picture of the Branch, the roots, as is the case with a tree, remain unseen. "No one has ever seen God" (John 1:18). But Jesus is the Branch, the proof that the root is there. "For in Christ all the fullness of the Deity lives in bodily form" (Colossians 2:9).

The picture then changes to a stone: "See, the stone I have set in front of Joshua! There are seven eyes on that one stone, and I will engrave an inscription on it."

The number 7 is often used as the number for completeness in the Bible. There were seven days in the first week. In the book of Revelation, John writes to the seven churches. The examples of 7 used in this way are many.

The footnote in the NIV suggests that the eyes are facets. This is possible. It is also possible that the Lord means just eyes.

In the next vision in chapter 4, we hear about the seven lights: "These seven are the eyes of the LORD, which range throughout the earth" (verse 10).

Sight is connected to this stone in an important way. Verse 9 of chapter 3 begins with the word "see." We are not sure of the meaning of the seven eyes, but they are eyes, and eyes see.

Jesus is pictured in many places as a stone, a rock. He is the rock upon which the church is built (Matthew 16:18). He is pictured as the cornerstone (Ephesians 2:20). Jesus even said about himself, "He who falls on this stone will be broken to pieces, but he on whom it falls will be crushed" (Matthew 21:44).

There is an inscription on the stone. In Revelation 2:17 God tells the church at Pergamum: "To him who overcomes, I will give some of the hidden manna. I will also give him a white stone with a new name written on it, known only to him who receives it."

The name Jesus was a name not known. It summed up the whole life's inscription of the one who carried it. Even the disciples, after Jesus' resurrection, wondered if perhaps he was going to restore the kingdom to Israel. The name was Jesus, and children in confirmation class are taught that the name of God is everything we know about God. We do not know what the inscription on the stone was, but we do know that it said something like the inscription written in the air on the day of Jesus' transfiguration: "This is my Son, whom I love. Listen to him!" (Mark 9:7).

We are bold to make the connection to Jesus and this stone with its inscription because of the words that Zechariah said: "I will remove the sin of this land in a single day" (verse 9). The inscription that day when God's Son did this was very clear. It was Pilate's writing, but it was God's will. JESUS OF NAZARETH, KING OF THE JEWS. And the one who bore that inscription said on that day, "It is finished." Paradise became possible for thieves and for us. Our King took away our sins in a single day.

Now to the final frame of the picture! The scene is full of good and contentment, the very picture of heaven. Peace pervades, the peace that passes understanding when the weight of our sins is lifted from our backs and souls as the result of this one day. Then we have the pleasure of the good, the ability to sit peacefully under our own fruit trees—shades of the picture God paints to us in the Revelation of John: "On each side of the river stood the tree of life, bearing twelve crops of fruit, yielding its fruit every month. And the leaves of the tree are for the healing of the nations" (Revelation 22:2).

What a chapter it is! Full of pictures! We see a burning stick, dirty clothes, rich clothes, the Branch, a stone, and a pastoral picture of peace.

The gold lampstand and the two olive trees

4 **Then the angel who talked with me returned and wakened me, as a man is wakened from his sleep. ²He asked me, "What do you see?"**

I answered, "I see a solid gold lampstand with a bowl at the top and seven lights on it, with seven channels to the lights. ³Also there are two olive trees by it, one on the right of the bowl and the other on its left."

⁴I asked the angel who talked with me, "What are these, my lord?"

⁵He answered, "Do you not know what these are?"

"No, my lord," I replied.

⁶So he said to me, "This is the word of the LORD to Zerubbabel: 'Not by might nor by power, but by my Spirit,' says the LORD Almighty.

⁷"What are you, O mighty mountain? Before Zerubbabel you will become level ground. Then he will bring out the capstone to shouts of 'God bless it! God bless it!'"

⁸Then the word of the LORD came to me: ⁹"The hands of Zerubbabel have laid the foundation of this temple; his hands will also complete it. Then you will know that the LORD Almighty has sent me to you.

¹⁰"Who despises the day of small things? Men will rejoice when they see the plumb line in the hand of Zerubbabel.

"(These seven are the eyes of the LORD, which range throughout the earth.)"

¹¹Then I asked the angel, "What are these two olive trees on the right and the left of the lampstand?"

¹²Again I asked him, "What are these two olive branches beside the two gold pipes that pour out golden oil?"

¹³He replied, "Do you not know what these are?"

"No, my lord," I said.

¹⁴So he said, "These are the two who are anointed to serve the Lord of all the earth."

Chapter 4 begins with Zechariah sleeping.

We might fancy that if we could see an angel, we would be so excited that we would never sleep again. But not so. The Russian writer Dostoevski said, "Man gets used to everything, the rascal." Zechariah ate angels' food and fell asleep! Disciples too fell asleep on the Mount of Transfiguration when Moses, Elijah, and Jesus were there in special appearance. Today the head of a man in the pew bobs and jerks during the sermon.

It is not that we lack enthusiasm for exciting things as believers in God. We have Moses and the prophets. They are more exciting, Abraham told the rich man in hell, than someone coming back from the dead to entertain us.

The angel tapped Zechariah on the shoulder and asked this question in muted tone: "What do you see?" The same question is asked time and again as the angel walks Zechariah through the visions. It is not enough to just see.

The one asking the question wants the one seeing to understand what it is he is seeing. In this case, the angel is the careful guide to the sights, and through his explanation, we see too.

We believe in angels. We *need* angels. They are not just something children believe in and adults speak of with condescending smiles. We depend on the angels for our safety. Even the devil realizes this. He quoted this very fact to Jesus during his temptation. And what he misquoted is true for Christians because we hear in Psalm 91, "He will command his angels concerning you to guard you in all your ways; they will lift you up in their hands, so that you will not strike your foot against a stone" (verses 11,12).

To the angel's question to Zechariah, "Do you not know what these are?" we too must say, "No, my lord." So the Lord speaks through the angel and tells us.

Basically, the vision was one of lights and the apparatus of lights. There was a solid gold lampstand (we have a 22-karat God!). There was some kind of bowl or basin on it, and there were seven lights. The lights were the lamps made of clay with their seven spouts, or channels, to the point of the flame. There were also two trees, olive trees.

This is explained at Zechariah's request: "This is the word of the Lord to Zerubbabel."

"[God's] word is a lamp to my feet and a light for my path" (Psalm 119:105). God himself makes the connection between light and his Word. It is like the light because it makes clear the way we should go. It points out the dangers along the way and outlines them in its light. The Word brings life, as light brings life to plants. It tells us what is coming in the future; it enlightens us. This was especially the case when the angel pointed out things that would happen in the future. We could say he cast light on the future.

The angel was quick to point out that the level ground in front of Zerubbabel was not there by accident or by Zerubbabel's engineering. "'Not by might nor by power, but by my Spirit,' says the LORD Almighty." In the context, it would not be overwhelming power on the part of the Jews that would establish and build the temple. It would be by God's power. "Unless the LORD builds the house, its builders labor in vain" (Psalm 127:1).

There was joy, however, in being allowed to participate in the building of God's house. Zerubbabel would move the capstone into place, and the words of dedication for the building and its purpose would be spoken: "God bless it! God bless it!" Believers in company with mortar and stone echo those same words whenever they dedicate a building to their Lord. "Men will rejoice when they see the plumb line in the hand of Zerubbabel."

God had spoken. The plans for building the temple were underway. Even the dedication loomed promisingly. And it all came about by small things. The Lord delighted (and still does!) in working with small things to accomplish his great things. It was a shepherd boy who toppled the giant Goliath. There was an unstated despising of small things when a disciple said, "Here is a boy with five small barley loaves and two small fish, but how far will they go among so many?" (John 6:9).

"Who despises the day of small things?" the angel asks. This temptation follows right down through the work of the church. The meek will inherit the earth. The humble and the uneducated will take the message to the learned and the wise. "Go into all the world and preach the good news to all creation" (Mark 16:15). Jesus said those words to 11 disciples. There number was small, but "God chose the weak things of the world to shame the strong. He chose the lowly things of this world and the despised things—and the things that are not—to nullify the things that are" (1 Corinthians 1:27,28).

Regarding the parenthetical remark in the last part of verse 10, see the explanation of chapter 3 verse 9.

The two olive trees are described as the "two who are anointed to serve the Lord of all the earth." These two trees seem to symbolize the priestly and royal offices, as represented by Joshua the priest and Zerubbabel, who was from the royal house of King David.

The flying scroll

5 I looked again—and there before me was a flying scroll!
²He asked me, "What do you see?"

I answered, "I see a flying scroll, thirty feet long and fifteen feet wide."

³And he said to me, "This is the curse that is going out over the whole land; for according to what it says on one side, every thief will be banished, and according to what it says on the other, everyone who swears falsely will be banished. ⁴The Lᴏʀᴅ Almighty declares, 'I will send it out, and it will enter the house of the thief and the house of him who swears falsely by my name. It will remain in his house and destroy it, both its timbers and its stones.'"

The picture of the flying scroll is not unlike that which comes to mind when a person at the county fair sees an airplane towing a message along behind it. Everyone looks up. Everyone sees it. It is a real eye-catcher.

The flying scroll that Zechariah saw also had odd proportions for a scroll. It was half as wide as it was long. The dimensions of two copper scrolls found at Qumran in the Holy Land were 12 inches wide by about 90 inches long. This seems to have been fairly representative of the dimensions of most scrolls (*The Dead Sea Scrolls,* William Sanford LaSor, 1956).

Another thing about the scroll that Zechariah saw, which we notice immediately, is that the scroll was huge! It was meant to be seen. And it was a curse, a preachment of law to two types of people—thieves and those who had sworn falsely.

The Lord God takes the offenses of the thieves and perjurers personally. As all of the commandments in one way or another do, the Seventh Commandment, which says not to steal, is directly connected with the First Commandment. People steal because they have not learned to trust the Lord their God above all things. Stealing is a sin of taking things into our own hands, literally and figuratively. The Lord is the one who distributes possessions, and he does this according to his love and wisdom. People steal presumably because they are dissatisfied with what they have. This is a serious matter that the scroll talked about. Stealing is telling God he has made a mistake in the distribution of possessions.

Perjury is also a serious crime, so serious that it merited inclusion on the flying scroll. In perjury God is implicated again; his good name is involved. "I swear to tell the truth, the whole truth, and nothing but the truth, so help me God." The Second Commandment comes especially into play here: "You shall not misuse the name of the LORD your God" (Exodus 20:7).

Human beings of the 21st century should not lose sight of the flying scroll of Zechariah. There still is a God in heaven who is very jealous of his name. He hears the senseless expletives. He knows each flippant misuse.

The punishment for the thief and perjurer will be like acid spending a night in a house, eating wood and stone alike. The word translated "it will remain" is really the word that means to spend the night or to sojourn. Dissatisfaction (stealing) and dishonesty (swearing falsely) are cancers that eat away at the person who traffics in them. They affect everything he has.

The woman in a basket

⁵Then the angel who was speaking to me came forward and said to me, "Look up and see what this is that is appearing."

⁶I asked, "What is it?"

He replied, "It is a measuring basket." And he added, "This is the iniquity of the people throughout the land."

⁷Then the cover of lead was raised, and there in the basket sat a woman! ⁸He said, "This is wickedness," and he pushed her back into the basket and pushed the lead cover down over its mouth.

⁹Then I looked up—and there before me were two women, with the wind in their wings! They had wings like those of a stork, and they lifted up the basket between heaven and earth.

¹⁰"Where are they taking the basket?" I asked the angel who was speaking to me.

¹¹He replied, "To the country of Babylonia to build a house for it. When it is ready, the basket will be set there in its place."

The dialogue between the angel and Zechariah continued. "What is it?" Zechariah asked. The angel answered, "It is a measuring basket."

This is the *ephah* that is mentioned often in the Old Testament. The word itself is of Egyptian extraction. Perhaps this was the measure used by Joseph's servants as they filled the granaries of Egypt during the seven good years and as they divided out the grain in the seven bad years. We are not certain today of its exact volume. It was a unit of measure, something like our bushel basket.

The iniquity of the people was being kept track of, measured.

A woman, who is the personification of wickedness, sat in the basket. It was a kind of Pandora's box. She sat under a good stout cover, one made of lead.

We notice that she was contained. She did not have free rein or sway in this world. Wickedness, though rampant, is contained by God. It is shackled. "We know that in all things God works for the good of those who love him, who have been called according to his purpose" (Romans 8:28). Perhaps, with this in mind, Luther was prompted to state that the devil is the greatest servant of the Lord. He works to accomplish God's will contrary to his own will. The devil is restrained in his activity. Otherwise even the elect would be taken. Job is evidence that the devil is curtailed in his activity. "'Does Job fear God for nothing?' Satan replied. 'Have you not put a hedge around him and his household and everything he has?'" (Job 1:10). In Revelation 20:2 we have the picture of an angel seizing the great dragon and binding him for one thousand years.

It is great news for us who cower when we hear the hellish lion roar to know that the lion is on a leash or, in the picture that we have before us in our text, that the wicked lady is in a basket with a lead cover on it.

Evil is not happy being confined. That is shown by the fact that when the basket was opened, the woman whose name was wickedness wanted out. She would have made it too if she had not been forcibly shoved back into the basket and sealed in with the lead cover.

Then women—wonderful women with wings like storks—performed the welcome work of removing the evil from the land and transporting it elsewhere.

They took it to the land of Shinar. That is the Hebrew word for the land that is translated as "Babylonia" here. Genesis chapters 10 and 11 tell us that Shinar was where people committed the atrocity of making a name for themselves and snubbing their noses at God. Babylon, with its evil reputation, was a proper place for the wicked lady.

The thing we wish to note is that God is going to rid the world of evil. The great purging is coming on judgment day, when the workers will gather the wheat and separate the chaff and weeds from it. On the other hand, it is already happening. Ananias and Sapphira are examples of wickedness taken out of the church. God did it. In 1 Corinthians chapter 11, in connection with the Lord's Supper and a misuse of it, Paul wrote, "That is why many among you are weak and sick, and a number of you have fallen asleep" (verse 30). In 1 John 2:19 we hear, "They went out from us, but they did not really belong to us."

God will not allow evil to continue to live among his people forever. His hand shoves it down into the basket, and the lead cover falls into place.

In the church evil cannot peacefully coexist with good. "Expel the wicked man from among you," said the apostle Paul to the congregation in Corinth (1 Corinthians 5:13). "What do righteousness and wickedness have in common? Or what fellowship can light have with darkness?" (2 Corinthians 6:14).

There is a final home for wickedness. It is prepared by God. "Depart from me, you who are cursed, into the eternal fire *prepared* for the devil and his angels" (Matthew 25:41).

The four chariots

6 **I looked up again—and there before me were four chariots coming out from between two mountains—mountains of bronze! ²The first chariot had red horses, the second black, ³the third white, and the fourth dappled—all of them powerful. ⁴I asked the angel who was speaking to me, "What are these, my lord?"**

⁵The angel answered me, "These are the four spirits of heaven, going out from standing in the presence of the Lord of the whole world. ⁶The one with the black horses is going toward the north country, the one with the white horses toward the west, and the one with the dappled horses toward the south."

⁷**When the powerful horses went out, they were straining to go throughout the earth. And he said, "Go throughout the earth!" So they went throughout the earth.**

⁸**Then he called to me, "Look, those going toward the north country have given my Spirit rest in the land of the north."**

The next vision is of chariots and the horses pulling them. The idea of chariots and horses is not a new picture. Elisha's servant saw fiery chariots surrounding Elisha and the people. They were for their protection (2 Kings 6:17). Elijah had been taken to heaven in a whirlwind that followed the fiery chariots. It even prompted Elisha to cry out, "My father! My father! The chariots and horsemen of Israel!" (2 Kings 2:12).

It is difficult, if not impossible, to attach any significance to the color of the horses strictly on the basis of what we read here in Zechariah. The book of Revelation, however, does speak of different colors of horses and lists the connection of the colors to what the colors represent. In chapter 6 it speaks of a white horse—white for conquest. We know that white is also a symbol of rightness and of purity. It speaks of a red horse—red for bloodshed and fighting. It speaks of a black horse—black for want and famine. It speaks of a pale horse (comparable to our spotted horse), signifying the awful paleness of death.

The horses were from heaven and they were strong. They appeared between bronze. They came from God to do his will on earth. It is, finally, true that death and destruction are the Lord's will too. "Whoever does not believe stands condemned" (John 3:18). These horses and chariots represent the four spirits of heaven, going out from standing in the presence of the Lord of the whole earth. It is a picture of majesty and power. The horses and chariots were anxious to do their work, even straining to do their work (verse 7).

If we can use the Revelation of John mentioned above to decode the colors of the horses, then the north and south particularly were hit hard. One got death, and the other got famine.

The physical enemies of God's people always came either from the land of the Tigris and Euphrates in the north or from Egypt and Philistia in the south. There is a God in heaven who vindicates his people and fights for them.

It is difficult to interpret verse 8 with a great deal of certainty from our place in history. Exactly how and when the spirit of God rested in the land we can't say. We can see from the book of Isaiah that God's spirit is also described as a spirit of judgment: "He will cleanse the bloodstains from Jerusalem by a spirit of judgment and a spirit of fire" (4:4). This certainly fits with the picture of judgment already drawn in the appearance of the chariots and horses and by the woman in the basket at the end of chapter 5.

A crown for Joshua

⁹The word of the LORD came to me: ¹⁰"Take silver and gold from the exiles Heldai, Tobijah and Jedaiah, who have arrived from Babylon. Go the same day to the house of Josiah son of Zephaniah. ¹¹Take the silver and gold and make a crown, and set it on the head of the high priest, Joshua son of Jehozadak. ¹²Tell him this is what the LORD Almighty says: 'Here is the man whose name is the Branch, and he will branch out from his place and build the temple of the LORD. ¹³It is he who will build the temple of the LORD, and he will be clothed with majesty and will sit and rule on his throne. And he will be a priest on his throne. And there will be harmony between the two.' ¹⁴The crown will be given to Heldai, Tobijah, Jedaiah and Hen son of Zephaniah as a memorial in the temple of the LORD. ¹⁵Those who are far away will come and help to build the temple of the LORD, and you will know that the LORD Almighty has sent me to you. This will happen if you diligently obey the LORD your God."

Verses 9 to 15 speak about coronation. Zechariah was to take gold and silver for the crown from people who returned from Babel (Babylonia). He was to fashion a crown and put it on the head of the high priest, Joshua. With the crowning comes a proclamation, a reference to the Branch.

Jesus is the only one who can fit the description of these verses. (See comments on the Branch in 3:8.) He had the duty of building the church, and it obviously wasn't just a physical temple that he was going to build. He looked at the physical temple in Jerusalem and said, "I will destroy this man-made temple" (Mark 14:58). Saint Matthew tells us, "Jesus left the temple and was walking away when his disciples came up to him to call his attention to its buildings. 'Do you see all these things?' he asked. 'I tell you the truth, not one stone here will be left on another; every one will be thrown down'" (24:1,2).

This is not to say that the temple building was unimportant. God himself made the plans for it. God commanded it to be built. But the temple of Solomon would have remained a meaningless monument of stone and cedar had not the glory of the Lord filled it and God taken up his residence there among his people. In the temple that Zechariah describes, "He will be clothed with majesty and will sit and rule on his throne. And he will be a priest on his throne."

The temple of the Lord would not be built with cold, dead stones but with living stones. We think of what Saint Peter wrote to Christians centuries later: "You also, like living stones, are being built into a spiritual house to be a holy priesthood, offering spiritual sacrifices acceptable to God through Jesus Christ" (1 Peter 2:5). John, by the miracle of revelation, actually saw this temple in a vision: "I did not see a temple in the city, because the Lord God Almighty and the Lamb are its temple" (Revelation 21:22). Jesus will gather those together who will be his glory, those whom he will live among for eternity.

Not only will Jesus gather them. He will use people to do it. "Those who are far away will come and help to build the temple of the LORD." World mission work is done. Today, even Third World countries are themselves sending missionaries. The prophecy of Zechariah is being fulfilled before our eyes!

Verse 13 speaks about the priest also ruling, and with the ruling there is harmony. There is no confusing the roles of church and state. The catechism explains this about Jesus when it describes his work as Prophet, *Priest, and King*. Priest and King—"He will be a priest on his throne"—seems like a mixed metaphor of church and state until we understand what the catechism and the Bible teach about Jesus' work.

"The crown will be given . . . as a memorial in the temple of the LORD." To which action we hear the echo of the refrain, "And he shall reign forever and ever!" We are reminded; our church is filled with things to remind us. The Lord's Supper is also "in remembrance of him." The stained-glass windows, the crucifix, the altar, and the colors of the vestments and altar cloths all serve to remind us.

We forget so easily.

The section closes with the words "This will happen if you diligently obey the LORD your God." In the Hebrew language the condition is stressed by saying, "If you really, really listen!" Obedience is really, really listening to the Word of God. Our lives exist properly on a careful, diligent obedience to God's Word. That seems self-evident to even a casual student of God's Word. But we find ourselves in trouble time and again because we slipped in this most important condition to happiness and success—did we listen, really?

PART TWO

The Second Word
(7:1–8:23)

Religion, but not for God?

7 **In the fourth year of King Darius, the word of the LORD came to Zechariah on the fourth day of the ninth month, the month of Kislev. ²The people of Bethel had sent Sharezer and Regem-Melech, together with their men, to entreat the LORD ³by asking the priests of the house of the LORD Almighty and the prophets, "Should I mourn and fast in the fifth month, as I have done for so many years?"**

⁴Then the word of the LORD Almighty came to me: ⁵"Ask all the people of the land and the priests, 'When you fasted and mourned in the fifth and seventh months for the past seventy years, was it really for me that you fasted? ⁶And when you were eating and drinking, were you not just feasting for yourselves? ⁷Are these not the words the LORD proclaimed through the earlier prophets when Jerusalem and its surrounding towns were at rest and prosperous, and the Negev and the western foothills were settled?'"

Two years had elapsed since the first word came to Zechariah from the Lord. The preacher continued to preach. The people continued to hear. God continued to manifest his will and patience to his people. The people were not yet in line with God's will as it becomes clear in this chapter. In verse 11 we hear, "They refused to pay attention."

In spite of continuing inattention on the part of God's people, the book goes on for seven more chapters. This is an example of God's patience. "If we are faithless, he will remain faithful, for he cannot disown himself" (2 Timothy 2:13).

The people sent an assembly to the prophet to find out something from God. In this we see the Old Testament way of getting a revelation. God had told them, "Go to the priest." He was the one who was in the middle, the one who represented the people's case to God and brought God's Word back to the people. The archetypes were Moses and Aaron. They spoke to the Lord for the people. The Lord commissioned them to do this. And they would speak to the people for God.

The New Testament and the priesthood of Jesus changed this. Jesus came as Prophet, Priest, and King. The book of Hebrews makes it clear that we do not have to follow the Old Testament procedure of having a human priest talk to God for us: "Because Jesus lives forever, he has a permanent priesthood. Therefore he is able to save completely those who come to God through him, because he always lives to intercede for them. Such a high priest meets our need—one who is holy, blameless, pure, set apart from sinners, exalted above the heavens. Unlike the other high priests, he does not need to offer sacrifices day after day, first for his own sins, and then for the sins of the people. He sacrificed for their sins once for all when he offered himself" (Hebrews 7:24-27).

The question that Sharezer and Regem-Melech brought to the Lord was, Should we continue with the mourning and fasting in the fifth month as we have in the past? Seventy years earlier it had been in the fifth month when Babylonian armies destroyed Jerusalem, including the beautiful temple of Solomon (2 Kings 25:8,9). Succeeding generations of Jews each year commemorated the anniversary of that tragedy as a day of national humiliation and prayer. Seventy years later, they came to Zechariah with this question: "Now that the new temple is nearing completion, should we continue to observe the anniversary of the old one's destruction?"

They got more of an answer than they had bargained for. The Lord answered, "When you fasted and mourned . . . was it really for me that you fasted?" In other words, if the fasting and mourning came from hearts made low because of a knowledge of sin, then the worship was acceptable to God. If, however, the tears were just tears of habit and not heart, the worship was an insult to God.

Speaking as a prophet of God, Joel said, "'Return to me with all your heart, with fasting and weeping and mourning.' Rend your heart and not your garments" (2:12,13). This is the implied message of Zechariah to his people too. "Your religion—is it for you or is it for God?" Is the practice a matter of the exterior or of the interior?

It may be that some go to church just for the discipline of it. Church attendance for them is like exercising, painful while you do it but feels great after it is over. Some may go to church for the image that a "churchgoer" enjoys in the community. (Some politicians even make a point of claiming this for themselves.) Some may go to church as a matter of culture. It is what their parents always did. They do it too, without really knowing why. Some possibly go to church for insurance—covering all the bases in life, just in case.

The Lord gives us all a good yardstick with which to measure our worship for him and to him. It comes to us in a simple question that we can and should ask ourselves when we prepare to worship: "Is what I am doing here done to the glory of God, or am I thinking primarily of myself?"

If we take stock of our faith and life and find that we have fallen short and the resulting shortage causes us grief in our hearts, then we are worshiping God properly. We are tearing our hearts and not our garments, as the prophet Joel told us to do.

The prophet Zechariah mentioned fasting in verse 5. If we could say in our hearts that we would forgo food for a day so that we might have more time to spend with God in prayer, we would be worshiping God and not ourselves. Even if we should fast for a day to discipline ourselves so that we might have better control over our flesh, this would be worshiping God and not doing the effort for ourselves. "Physical training is of some value" (1 Timothy 4:8). Thanksgiving, Christmas, and Easter can be special holidays of worship to our God. They can also become just occasions for friendly festivity. God's name is sometimes mentioned before the turkey is eaten and never heard again all day. Should this be the case? The Lord would question rightfully, "When you were eating and drinking, were you not just feasting for yourselves?"

Verse 7 is the gentle reminder that this is not the first time the Lord has mentioned hollow worship. The prophets have always warned against this. "I desire mercy, not sacrifice" is the recurring message (Hosea 6:6). Jesus quoted Isaiah and warned, "These people honor me with their lips, but their hearts are far from me. They worship me in vain" (Matthew 15:8,9).

Hard hearts

⁸And the word of the Lord came again to Zechariah: ⁹"This is what the Lord Almighty says: 'Administer true justice; show mercy and compassion to one another. ¹⁰Do not oppress the widow or the fatherless, the alien or the poor. In your hearts do not think evil of each other.'

¹¹"But they refused to pay attention; stubbornly they turned their backs and stopped up their ears. ¹²They made their hearts as hard as flint and would not listen to the law or to the words that the LORD Almighty had sent by his Spirit through the earlier prophets. So the LORD Almighty was very angry.

¹³" 'When I called, they did not listen; so when they called, I would not listen,' says the LORD Almighty. ¹⁴"I scattered them with a whirlwind among all the nations, where they were strangers. The land was left so desolate behind them that no one could come or go. This is how they made the pleasant land desolate.' "

Verses 8 to 10 are a continuation of the theme that has been set for this chapter. They contain a description of true worship. It is striking to note that true religion, as God prescribes it, is not done to God but to our neighbor. Every single thing that God wanted the people (and us) to do here is something that was directed toward our neighbor. "If anyone says, 'I love God,' yet hates his brother, he is a liar. For anyone who does not love his brother, whom he has seen, cannot love God, whom he has not seen. . . . Whoever loves God must also love his brother" (1 John 4:20,21).

The directives of verses 9 and 10 can be summarized in three commands: (1) be fair, (2) be merciful, (3) be compassionate.

The Lord's eye was on the law courts of the land. He was concerned for the person who "got taken." These people were *his* people! It stirred him to righteous anger when others took advantage of them. In wisdom and love he gave the poor their belongings, however small or poor they appeared to be. The Lord was the one who answered the requests of the poor that came to him within the confines of the Fourth Petition of the prayer he would later teach his disciples to pray: "Give us today our daily bread" (Matthew 6:11). Martin Luther explained that our daily bread is "all that we need for our body and life." The poor and deprived among God's ancient people *needed* these things even more than others. Defrauding them was doubly bad.

Mercy and compassion were also matters that applied here. If someone really felt mercy, he would not take advantage of the widows or the orphans. Instead he would help them and share with them from the sustenance that God provided. In a word, he would be compassionate.

The Hebrews had a vivid picture before them when they heard the word we know as *compassion*. Their word was related to the word for the womb. Compassion is the feeling that a mother has for her children, who are part of her own body. Blood is thicker than water. When someone we love and care for is hurting, we hurt too, in the pits of our stomachs. Compassion can actually hurt. We *feel* for each other.

The Lord described the religion of the last days as being such in which "the love of most will grow cold" (Matthew 24:12). Romans chapter 1 describes wicked people as "senseless, faithless, heartless, ruthless" (verse 31). Zechariah said to God's people in general, regardless of their age in history, "Show mercy and compassion to one another."

Mercy also has to do with our feelings for each other. "In your hearts do not think evil of each other." Mercy gently rubs out the wrinkles caused by infractions, either real or imagined. Mercy puts the best construction possible on our neighbor's actions. Mercy forgives and tries to forget. The Lord simply said, "Don't do it! Do not think evil of each other in the convenient chamber of your heart. Don't do it!"

Verses 11 and 12 hold the response to the Lord's gentle request for true worship: "They refused." God told his people the right way, but they refused. "How often I have longed to gather your children together, as a hen gathers her chicks under her wings, *but you were not willing*" (Matthew 23:37). When the Lord spoke to his people, backs turned, ears stopped, and hearts became flint hard. What a picture of man's reluctance and rebellion! And there without the grace of God are we.

"So the LORD Almighty was very angry." This was not a stewing, old grandfatherly god rocking perplexed in his chair and pleading in a quavery voice to naughty grandchildren. This was the *Almighty* with his nostrils flaring in anger and with the awful capability to wreak destruction on those who turned their shoulders and tempered their hearts.

By itself, sin is an abstract thing. It does not exist outside of living beings. It turns God's creation into a hateful person. God is angry with people! Hell is proof of this. But he loves people with an even greater intensity. That is a seeming contradiction which only the cross of Christ can bridge. The cross is the piece of the puzzle that joins God's intense anger and his intense love. He damned his Son to die because of the one; he saved us from death because of the other.

The further result of the people's hard hearts was that when they called on God, he wasn't available. Prayer is an invitation to talk to God. "Call upon me in the day of trouble; I will deliver you, and you will honor me" (Psalm 50:15). This is the invitation from God, and the Second Commandment tells us how to use God's name rightfully. But the fact remains that for those who refuse him, there will come a time when they will call but he will not answer. He stands ready for a long time, but even a long time comes to an end. There is that awful time when the prayer, no matter how sincere or urgent, is not heard anymore. There is that awful, aching echo of nothingness that Jesus felt when he said, "My God, my God, why have you forsaken me?" (Matthew 27:46).

Verses 13 and 14 describe the desolation caused by a hard heart. As a hurricane scatters, this is what happens.

"This is how they made the pleasant land desolate." This was the manual to self-destruction. This was how a person acted to change life into a howling waste devoid of anything pleasant. The way of the sinner is hard. It leads to a scorching land where the sky is bronze and the earth is brass.

The Lord promises to bless Jerusalem with old age and youth

8 Again the word of the LORD Almighty came to me. ²This is what the LORD Almighty says: "I am very jealous for Zion; I am burning with jealousy for her."

³This is what the LORD says: "I will return to Zion and dwell in Jerusalem. Then Jerusalem will be called the City of Truth, and the mountain of the LORD Almighty will be called the Holy Mountain."

⁴This is what the LORD Almighty says: "Once again men and women of ripe old age will sit in the streets of Jerusalem, each with cane in hand because of his age. ⁵The city streets will be filled with boys and girls playing there."

⁶This is what the LORD Almighty says: "It may seem marvelous to the remnant of this people at that time, but will it seem marvelous to me?" declares the LORD Almighty.

⁷This is what the LORD Almighty says: "I will save my people from the countries of the east and the west. ⁸I will bring them back to live in Jerusalem; they will be my people, and I will be faithful and righteous to them as their God."

In the 23 verses of chapter 8, the statement "This is what the LORD Almighty says" is repeated ten times. And twice, in verses 1 and 18, Zechariah says, "Again the word of the LORD Almighty came to me." One of the proofs for the inspiration of the Bible is just this fact: the Bible *claims* to be the Word of Israel's covenant God. The testimony almost labors in this chapter. Twelve direct references to this being God's Word in these few verses! God is making a point.

Usually we hear the word *jealous* in a bad context. Usually the one who is jealous is at fault. But in verse 2 the Savior-God calls himself jealous: "I am very jealous for Zion; I am burning with jealousy for her." His people brought him to righteous jealousy. He did not want them flirting with other gods. He means business with his First Commandment.

This anthropomorphism of God being the jilted lover is one we all understand clearly, and the Bible uses it often throughout its pages. History is woven full of examples of men and women vying for each other's complete love and reacting with different expressions of jealousy when the love they wanted got waylaid. Disappointed love causes such acute feelings. "I am burning with jealousy for her."

But isn't it a great thing to know? True, we do not want to make God jealous and see him burn with jealousy. But, at the same time, it is a comfort to know he can get jealous over us. No one gets jealous over someone he has no love for. An object of disdain or disgust stirs up no feelings of jealousy in us. But one we love dearly and want for our own, one we cannot stand the thought of losing to another causes us to be jealous. And so it is with God. He loves us so much he can't stand the thought of losing us to some false lover. His love is so great that he even comes looking for us when we have been unfaithful to him. His sense of jealousy is sharper and fiercer than ours; his forgiveness spans greater canyons of transgression than ours. He even forgives us when we cannot forgive ourselves. "This then is how we know that we belong to the truth, and how we set our hearts at rest in his presence whenever our hearts condemn us. For God is greater than our hearts, and he knows everything" (1 John 3:19,20).

79

The truth of this last statement rests on the evidence of verse 3. "I will return to Zion and dwell in Jerusalem." God came back. We sing these words: "Thou hast not left me oft as I left thee. On to the close, O Lord, abide with me" (CW 588:4). The result of God's coming back was that the foundation of peace (which is what *Jerusalem* means) was once more coupled with those two lovely words, truth and holiness. Jerusalem knew truth; Mount Zion knew holiness. Both were a picture of God's beloved, his church. To know once more what *true* love is! To stand before the Bridegroom in white and have it signify the truth—completely forgiven and clean! "Faultless to stand before his throne" (CW 382:4). What a great Advent thought these words are. Our King is coming, and he will love us!

The city of God's people will be lovely, lovely because of the only thing that can make a city lovely—people! The old will be there with canes in their hands. War and violence and disease will not snatch their lives away. They will be able to say with the psalmist, "I was young and now I am old, yet I have never seen the righteous forsaken or their children begging bread" (Psalm 37:25). And the young will be there too! There will be games, laughter, and energy. There will be exuberance of youth! What a fine place—a lovely place—where God will live with his people.

Is it too good to be true?

"'It may seem marvelous to the remnant of this people at that time, but will it seem marvelous to me?' declares the LORD Almighty." It was a rhetorical question. The answer was no. No, it was not just a dream! The miracle would happen. With God all things are possible.

Sometimes it is discouraging to be a remnant. True believers seem to be such a pitifully small group, clinging to each other in fear, wondering what is going to happen to them and their church. Promising people come into the church for a while and then are slain by some sword of the devil—they become disillusioned; the church appears too straightlaced for them; they say Christians are hypocritical. And they leave. The youth are confirmed and drop forever out of sight. The old standbys sometimes are also poisoned and go their separate ways. Yet the promise remains. There will be the old tried and true and the young full of pep and promise. This is God's church. The people will come from the east and the west, as he promises in verse 7.

Verse 8 is surprising. In view of all the good things God had done for them, we would expect that the people would promise to be faithful and righteous to God. Certainly he deserved their pledge. But no! *He* promised to be faithful and righteous to them! They were his people. They were saved by grace without any merit or worthiness on their parts. God came to them. They did not come to him. He brought them to himself; they didn't find the way there by themselves.

The Lord promises to bless Jerusalem with social prosperity

⁹**This is what the Lᴏʀᴅ Almighty says: "You who now hear these words spoken by the prophets who were there when the foundation was laid for the house of the Lᴏʀᴅ Almighty, let your hands be strong so that the temple may be built. ¹⁰Before that time there were no wages for man or beast. No one could go about his business safely because of his enemy, for I had turned every man against his neighbor. ¹¹But now I will not deal with the remnant of this people as I did in the past," declares the Lᴏʀᴅ Almighty.**

Verses 9 to 17 have a different theme than the one heard up to this time. A change was coming. God was hard on his people in the past; at this point he was going to have mercy. "So will I save you, and you will be a blessing" (verse 13).

As mentioned at the beginning of this book, Zechariah was a contemporary of Haggai. Together they had witnessed the return of the nation of Judah from captivity in far-off Babylon. They had also been witnesses when discouragement and a spirit of defeatism had shut down the temple-rebuilding project. Verse 9 refers to this fact: "You who now hear these words spoken by the prophets who were there when the foundation was laid for the house of the LORD Almighty."

In effect, the Lord was saying, "Listen to your preachers!" His will and word to the people came via prophets. The people could hear. God was speaking to them through the mouths of the prophets. The prophets had seen the foundation laid for the temple. They also had the Word of the Lord to direct the future building of the temple.

Their message was, "Let your hands be strong so that the temple may be built." This is the Hebrew way of saying, "Be encouraged!" We read these lovely words of 1 Samuel 23:16 in the King James Version: "And Jonathan Saul's son arose, and went to David into the wood, and strengthened his hand in God." And during the discouraging times he faced in the rebuilding of the wall around Jerusalem, Nehemiah said, "They [the enemies] were all trying to frighten us, thinking, 'Their hands will get too weak for the work, and it will not be completed.' But I prayed, 'Now strengthen my hands'" (6:9).

The one with strong hands, the one truly encouraged, is the one who has his hand in the hand of the Savior. When the prophets encouraged God's people to have strong hands and be encouraged, they were not suggesting that it be a home study or a do-it-yourself project.

Moses, leading the millions single-handedly, prayed, "May the favor of the Lord our God rest upon us; establish the work of our hands for us—yes, establish the work of our hands" (Psalm 90:17). Nothing is single-handed when God's hands strengthen our hands.

Verse 10 describes chaos and anarchy. There was no currency. There was no trust (upon which currency is based). No one was able to pay wages; consequently, no one could earn them. And the whole situation was caused by the Lord! The prophet Amos agreed when he said, "When disaster comes to a city, has not the LORD caused it?" (3:6). We read, "[The LORD] had turned every man against his neighbor."

Why?

How could God be so mean and vindictive?

This question, which borders on the blasphemous, is just the question that human beings ask when faced with the frightening prospects of a God who punishes for transgressions against his law and who lets people suffer the consequences of their actions. Human beings do not police the laws of God. He does. Vengeance is his; he will repay.

But there is also mercy. "'I will not deal with the remnant of this people as I did in the past,' declares the LORD Almighty." Social prosperity is once more in the offing.

The Lord promises to bless Jerusalem with good crops

[12]**"The seed will grow well, the vine will yield its fruit, the ground will produce its crops, and the heavens will drop their dew. I will give all these things as an inheritance to the remnant of this people. [13]As you have been an object of cursing among the nations, O Judah and Israel, so will I save you, and you will be a blessing. Do not be afraid, but let your hands be strong."**

Verses 12 and 13 show in a beautiful picture the mercy of God. The picture is couched in agricultural terms. The people of Zechariah's day were farmers. They understood. The best picture a farmer could imagine was good weather and good crops. This was his success and prosperity. This was life in the seven years of abundance in Pharaoh's dream.

Perhaps today we lose sight of this fact. We have always had an abundance of food. It comes to us wrapped in plastic, encased in brightly-colored cardboard. It stands many rows deep on crowded grocery-store shelves. But our food does not come from the supermarket. It comes from the ground. And it still comes to us because the Lord causes the rain and dew to fall from heaven and because he makes the seed germinate.

Food is a blessing. Food is life. In our portly society, food almost has become something we look upon as a curse. But verse 13 points out that the curse comes when there is famine in the land. (Among the Bantu of southern Africa, where famine is common and food remains precious, a common greeting is, "What are you eating these days?")

The heathen world curses God's people as the bully Goliath cursed the shepherd-boy David. But enough of it! God will save, and he will make his people a blessing and a cause for blessing. They will be the salt and light of the earth.

Let our hands be strong!

The Lord promises to bless Jerusalem with happy worship

¹⁴**This is what the LORD Almighty says: "Just as I had deter-mined to bring disaster upon you and showed no pity when your fathers angered me," says the LORD Almighty, ¹⁵"so now I have determined to do good again to Jerusalem and Judah. Do not be afraid. ¹⁶These are the things you are to do: Speak the truth to each other, and render true and sound judgment in your courts;**

¹⁷do not plot evil against your neighbor, and do not love to swear falsely. I hate all this," declares the LORD.

¹⁸Again the word of the LORD Almighty came to me. ¹⁹This is what the LORD Almighty says: "The fasts of the fourth, fifth, seventh and tenth months will become joyful and glad occasions and happy festivals for Judah. Therefore love truth and peace."

²⁰This is what the LORD Almighty says: "Many peoples and the inhabitants of many cities will yet come, ²¹and the inhabitants of one city will go to another and say, 'Let us go at once to entreat the LORD and seek the LORD Almighty. I myself am going.' ²²And many peoples and powerful nations will come to Jerusalem to seek the LORD Almighty and to entreat him."

²³This is what the LORD Almighty says: "In those days ten men from all languages and nations will take firm hold of one Jew by the hem of his robe and say, 'Let us go with you, because we have heard that God is with you.'"

The final verses of chapter 8, from verse 18 through verse 23, form one last entreaty to worship. As has been the case throughout chapter 8, the Lord is referred to as "Almighty." We remember that this is the Lord of Sabaoth, the Lord of hosts. He is the one over all. The one true God reared up from his throne of power and spoke: "This is what the LORD says—Israel's King and Redeemer, the LORD Almighty: I am the first and I am the last; apart from me there is no God" (Isaiah 44:6).

Verse 19 promised that the religious fasts would be joyful events for the people. It had to be this way. The fasting was worship for the God who worked good in their lives. They were privileged to call this God their own. They could proclaim this message by their fasting.

True worship has always been a happy, glad occurrence in the lives of God's people. There is a place for skipping and dancing before the ark of God, as David did. And if a hallelujah should issue out of the back pew of the church on Sunday, we should not necessarily grow uncomfortable.

That might not be our style, but maybe it should be. Pity the worshipers that have no joy—the kind of joy that cannot be contained. Beating the breast is to be a part of worship too. This is the way the humble tax collector worshiped in the back of the church. But it does not end this way. God's people go home forgiven. They receive forgiveness full and free. There must be joy! There must be the joy that surfaces and bubbles over in glad noise and action.

The verse ends with two important words—*truth* and *peace*. Happy worshipers love these two words.

The word in Hebrew for *truth* is the word *amen*. Used at the end of worship or at the end of prayer, it says that what has proceeded is true. Because it is true, the worshiper claims it for his own. Worship of the true God claims this for itself. It is truth for all people, as verses 20 to 22 tell. This dispels the notion that our faith is true for some but not for others. It is true for all, take it or leave it. Jesus said, "Everyone on the side of truth listens to me" (John 18:37).

The word for peace is the familiar *shalom*. Jews today use it for a greeting. We need peace that passes understanding. Martin Luther spoke about this peace in the Large Catechism when he spoke of the Fourth Petition: "Our life requires not only food and clothing and other necessities for our body, but also peace and concord. . . . Although we have received from God all good things in abundance, we cannot retain any of them or enjoy them in security and happiness unless he gives us a stable, peaceful government. For where dissension, strife, and war prevail, there our daily bread is taken away, or at least reduced."

We love peace. All worshipers of God love it and desire it—and have it! The church is spoken of as "Jerusalem." *Jerusalem* has the word *peace* in it—"foundation of peace." What a beautiful picture of the church. Zechariah knew the importance of the picture. He closed the verse with this request: "Therefore love truth and peace." It was not just an invitation. It was a command, the same kind of command the apostle Paul made when he told the congregation at Thessalonica, "Live in peace with each other" (1 Thessalonians 5:13). This was a carefully patrolled peace.

Verses 20 to 22 contain the dialogue of would-be-worshipers among themselves. They talked to each other city to city. There was an invitation and a resolve among them all: "Let us go at once to entreat the Lord and seek the Lord Almighty. I myself am going."

In Hebrew the literal translation of the people's resolve to entreat the Lord is, "Let us stroke the Lord's face." This is an idiom for appeasing someone's anger. These worshipers were concerned that the Lord not remain angry with them. They realized that he was angry and had just cause for being angry. Psalm 7 says, "God is angry *with the wicked* every day" (KJV), and the prophet Hosea warns of an angry God, who says: "I will tear them to pieces and go away; I will carry them off, with no one to rescue them. Then I will go back to my place until they admit their guilt. And they will seek my face" (5:14,15).

What a wonderful tribute God's people have in verse 23. Strangers come and grab them by the corner of their robes and say to them, "Let us go with you, because we have heard that God is with you." This is the ultimate in compliments. The word got around that the Lord was with his people. When the night is black and the only fire is the one in the camp of God's people, the people come like moths. "We have heard that God is with you."

This is mission work *par excellence!* It was more than the people having "In God We Trust" stamped on their small change. It was not done with great programs and strategies.

It was done when God's people lived as God's people. Then people saw and wanted that difference for themselves.

This is an exciting idea. And it is true, as the Ethiopian eunuch and the Philippian jailer proved. They bounded in and said, "What must I do to be saved?" They wanted it. They asked for it. The prophecy came true. They grabbed one Jew by the corner of his robe and said, "Let us go with you, because we have heard that God is with you."

The sad thing, of course, is that just being a Jew is not enough. Jews who turned their backs on God were shipped away to oblivion. Then no one asked them anymore if they could walk with them. The fire was no longer there.

We may call ourselves Christians, but unless we have a hold on the corner of the robe of Jesus, it makes no difference. We have no attraction. Our only attraction is with him! With him in our lives, people will hear and come, and the truth of Zechariah chapter 8 will be proven true once more.

The next section begins the oracles of Zechariah. These oracles are words of prophecy about coming events. The prophet is living up to his name; he is peering into the future.

PART THREE

The Prophecies of the Messianic King
(9:1–14:21)

Judgment on Israel's enemies

An Oracle

9 The word of the LORD is against the land of Hadrach
and will rest upon Damascus—
for the eyes of men and all the tribes of Israel
are on the LORD—
² and upon Hamath too, which borders on it,
and upon Tyre and Sidon, though they are very skillful.
³ Tyre has built herself a stronghold;
she has heaped up silver like dust,
and gold like the dirt of the streets.
⁴ But the Lord will take away her possessions
and destroy her power on the sea,
and she will be consumed by fire.
⁵ Ashkelon will see it and fear;
Gaza will writhe in agony,
and Ekron too, for her hope will wither.
Gaza will lose her king
and Ashkelon will be deserted.
⁶ Foreigners will occupy Ashdod,
and I will cut off the pride of the Philistines.
⁷ I will take the blood from their mouths,
the forbidden food from between their teeth.
Those who are left will belong to our God
and become leaders in Judah,
and Ekron will be like the Jebusites.

> **8 But I will defend my house
> against marauding forces.
> Never again will an oppressor overrun my people,
> for now I am keeping watch.**

The first oracle of this section deals with the Mediterranean seacoast and its inhabitants. These were often scourges of God's people. From the southern seacoast came the Philistines, and from the northern coast came the rich traders of Tyre and Sidon.

The prophecy of this encouraging word to God's people is threefold. It speaks against the inhabitants of Syria (Damascus, Hadrach, and Hamath), Phoenicia (Tyre and Sidon), and Philistia (Ashkelon, Gaza, and Ekron). These countries bordered God's people to the northwest, the north, and the south. Hadrach, mentioned only this one time in the Bible, has been lost to known history. It was someplace in Syria. Hamath is on the Orontes River. The cities of Tyre and Sidon were separated by about 20 miles. In Solomon's time there were agreements and treaties in existence between these cities and God's people. In fact, materials from these cities found their way into the temple at Jerusalem.

Tyre and Sidon were rich cities, but their riches had separated them from the true God. As Jesus in the New Testament would maintain about the rich entering heaven, it was also hard in the Old Testament for a rich man to enter the kingdom of heaven. Silver was in heaps, and gold was like dirt. That is how Zechariah saw it. The Lord said, "Where your treasure is, there your heart will be also" (Matthew 6:21). The heart of Tyre and Sidon was metallic. It would melt in the fire of God's judgment. In 332 B.C. Alexander the Great came and Tyre, the rock, fell quickly. Its name in Hebrew is *Tzor,* which means "rock." But as

God's people already sang, "Who is God besides the LORD? And who is the Rock except our God?" (Psalm 18:31).

Philistia too would feel God's judgment. The picture is graphic. There would be writhing in fear and empty, echoing cities where there were once strong people. There would be "foreigners" in Ashdod (verse 6). The word actually means "illegitimate children." There would be no kingly line or pure race anymore. There would only be ragtag settlers prowling among the ruins.

Verse 7 promises that false religion and its practices would be gone. Baal worship was the awful sin of Philistia, and it polluted God's people too. Samson not only flirted with the Philistine women; he flirted with the Philistine gods as well.

But the day was coming when the true faith would win out. The impostor gods would all be shown to be just that. The God of heaven would summon all of his people, and they would reign with him unmolested and undisturbed forever. "At the name of Jesus every knee should bow, in heaven and on earth and under the earth, and every tongue confess that Jesus Christ is Lord, to the glory of God the Father" (Philippians 2:10,11).

The Jebusites, original inhabitants of Jerusalem, of verse 7 were Canaanites. Genesis chapter 10 says that they were from Canaan's strain. Actually, Jebus was another name for Jerusalem. Joshua 15:63 tells us, "Judah could not dislodge the Jebusites, who were living in Jerusalem; to this day the Jebusites live there with the people of Judah." In 2 Samuel 5:6,7 we learn that David did take final control of Jebus (Jerusalem). The taunt of the Jebusites from their supposedly strong walls was, "You will not get in here; even the blind and the lame can ward you off" (verse 6). But their sarcasm was to no avail. The enemies of God's people toppled from their strong walls. Ekron is pictured as doing this too in verse 7 of Zechariah.

Verse 8 is the close of this frame of the prophecy. It is a beautiful picture of the Lord as watchman. He camps around his people with his armed hosts. "O little flock, fear not the Foe," a hymnist wrote (TLH 263:1). We think of Elisha's servant who cried out in fear at the sight of the enemy surrounding him and his master in the little town of Dothan. Elisha prayed to God, "'O LORD, open his eyes so he may see.' Then the LORD opened the servant's eyes, and he looked and saw the hills full of horses and chariots of fire all around Elisha" (2 Kings 6:17).

"For now I am keeping watch," is the closing word of the Lord. It was true for Zechariah's people, and today we continue to sleep in peace.

The coming of Zion's King

> 9 Rejoice greatly, O Daughter of Zion!
> Shout, Daughter of Jerusalem!
> See, your king comes to you,
> righteous and having salvation,
> gentle and riding on a donkey,
> on a colt, the foal of a donkey.
> 10 I will take away the chariots from Ephraim
> and the war-horses from Jerusalem,
> and the battle bow will be broken.
> He will proclaim peace to the nations.
> His rule will extend from sea to sea
> and from the River to the ends of the earth.
> 11 As for you, because of the blood of my covenant with you,
> I will free your prisoners from the waterless pit.
> 12 Return to your fortress, O prisoners of hope;
> even now I announce that I will restore twice as much
> to you.
> 13 I will bend Judah as I bend my bow
> and fill it with Ephraim.

**I will rouse your sons, O Zion,
     against your sons, O Greece,
     and make you like a warrior's sword.**

These words remind us of Advent. Verse 9 is often used as an Advent text. Here, hidden in the words of Zechariah, is a prophecy of Jesus coming into Jerusalem on Palm Sunday as King. It is also a reference for all Christians to the final fulfillment of prophecy, when the Lord comes again victoriously with all of his angels. Then the streets of heavenly Jerusalem will ring with the shouts of the victors. Shouting is impressive, and in our day and age we do much of it. Shouting thrives at sporting events. Imagine any kind of athletic game played without shouting. Would the effort even be any fun at all if there was no shouting? People shout themselves hoarse. From their living rooms they even shout at a glass screen that mirrors an event taking place hundreds of miles away!

Imagine the shouting and rejoicing that is going to take place when the Lord comes for his people! All Christians will rise up and shout themselves hoarse in exploding enthusiasm. God has come just as he said he would!

"*See*, your king," the verse says. We are going to see him. Just like Job we are going to see: "I know that my Redeemer lives, and that in the end he will stand upon the earth. And after my skin has been destroyed, yet in my flesh I will see God; I myself will see him with my own eyes—I, and not another" (Job 19:25-27).

We cannot look at the one picture of Jesus coming on Palm Sunday without also thinking of his second coming, which we too will witness along with all people. We say this particularly as we look at the scope of the peace that will accompany his arrival. It will be universal. There will no longer be any war chariots or battle bows. Pruning hooks and plowshares will take the place of swords and spears. This peace will come upon those people on the King's side. Real peace comes in knowing that you have won and that the other side is forever incapable of fighting.

The peace comes in rightness and righteousness. When the cause is finally shown without a doubt to be the right one, when believers finally see the fulfillment of all their hopes and dreams, then true peace of mind and heart will arrive.

It does not seem possible that meek, humble Jesus will bring the rampant forces of evil to unconditional surrender. It takes faith to accept this King *now*. It will not take faith to believe in him as King when he returns in the clouds of heaven to claim undisputed rule. But it will be forever too late for those who wait until that day to try and claim him as their King. "Look, he is coming with the clouds, and every eye will see him, even those who pierced him" (Revelation 1:7).

It will be a universal peace that will reach the east and west, north and south—all brought into the peace of God through the blood of the Son, all won through the agreement instigated by God himself: "God so loved the world that he gave his one and only Son" (John 3:16). Those were the divinely established terms of the covenant. "God was pleased to have all his fullness dwell in him, and through him to reconcile to himself all things, whether things on earth or things in heaven, by making peace through his blood, shed on the cross" (Colossians 1:19,20). Truly, as verse 11 of Zechariah says, "Because of the blood of my covenant with you." That is the only reason for peace—then or now.

The prisoners would also have this peace. It will be a peace of release for those in waterless pits. God is a God who rescues his people—like Jeremiah, Daniel, Joseph—out of pits from which they could never escape by themselves. Never mind if the pit is of our own or of others' digging; never mind whether the pit is physical or spiritual. We can return to the fortress, the Mighty Fortress, to the unbreachable place of safety and security.

God's people were prisoners of hope. Their hold had just about slipped. They were just about gone. The flame had just about died. But as long as there was life, there was hope. Sad words were spoken many years later on the road to Emmaus by two disciples fresh from the crucifixion of their Lord, "We had hoped that he was the one who was going to redeem Israel" (Luke 24:21). Life itself was lived by this hope. Without this hope, life was and is not worth living.

"*Even now* I announce that I will restore twice as much to you." The mind has trouble comprehending the goodness of God. Not only did he release the people from prison, but he also promised that they would receive twice as much good as they had previously received evil in their languishing. The words come to the people in a tone similar to the prophet Isaiah's words: "Comfort, comfort my people, says your God. Speak tenderly to Jerusalem, and proclaim to her that her hard service has been completed, that her sin has been paid for, that she has received from the LORD's hand *double for all her sins*" (Isaiah 40:1,2).

The goodness of God to his people is the theme upon which they will sing for eternity without ever tiring of it or exhausting its possibilities. What a King! No wonder the people line the streets to shout their praise and happiness! The section ends in martial tone. The Lord himself breaks back the bow. His keen eye looks down the straight arrow at the enemy; his muscles bunch for perfect release of the arrow. We can see a trace of a smile on the archer's face. Judah is the bow. Ephraim is the arrow. In the hands of the Lord they will prove deadly against the enemy. In his hands they will make telling shots. They fly straight and true.

What a bold picture! The Lord will use his church as his instrument in conquering the gentile world and bringing them into his family.

The Lord will appear

> ¹⁴ Then the LORD will appear over them;
>   his arrow will flash like lightning.
> The Sovereign LORD will sound the trumpet;
>   he will march in the storms of the south,
> ¹⁵   and the LORD Almighty will shield them.
> They will destroy
>   and overcome with slingstones.
> They will drink and roar as with wine;
>   they will be full like a bowl
>   used for sprinkling the corners of the altar.
> ¹⁶ The LORD their God will save them on that day
>   as the flock of his people.
> They will sparkle in his land
>   like jewels in a crown.
> ¹⁷ How attractive and beautiful they will be!
>   Grain will make the young men thrive,
>   and new wine the young women.

Verses 14 and 15 continue to picture the Warrior. The arrow flashes, the trumpet screams out, the shield comes up solidly, and the slingstones sail out with their deadly whir. God's people are a force to be reckoned with. "The LORD their God will save them on that day." We can hear it against a powerful backdrop of organ music: "With might of ours can naught be done; soon were our loss effected. But for us fights the valiant one whom God himself elected. You ask,

'Who is this?' Jesus Christ it is, the almighty Lord. And there's no other God; he holds the field forever" (CW 200:2).

The picture turns softly from the martial to the pastoral. The green pastures and quiet waters steal quietly over our senses. The sounds of war fade. Peaceful quiet reigns. God's people are with their Lord. The sins and struggles are gone. Instead of objects of disdain, the riffraff and scum of the world, God's people are objects of priceless worth and beauty. It must be so! God values his people so much that he gave his Son for them. The Lord's judgment of beauty and worth is good. He makes no errors when it comes to value. "How attractive and beautiful they will be!"

The Lord will care for Judah

10 Ask the LORD for rain in the springtime;
    it is the LORD who makes the storm clouds.
He gives showers of rain to men,
    and plants of the field to everyone.
² The idols speak deceit,
    diviners see visions that lie;
they tell dreams that are false,
    they give comfort in vain.
Therefore the people wander like sheep
    oppressed for lack of a shepherd.

³ "My anger burns against the shepherds,
    and I will punish the leaders;
for the LORD Almighty will care
    for his flock, the house of Judah,
    and make them like a proud horse in battle.
⁴ From Judah will come the cornerstone,
    from him the tent peg,
    from him the battle bow,
    from him every ruler.
⁵ Together they will be like mighty men
    trampling the muddy streets in battle.
Because the LORD is with them,
    they will fight and overthrow the horsemen.

When the rains do not come in southern Africa, the people head for special groves of trees, almost like shrines, where they pray to spirits to cause the rain to come. Many heathen people had this idea and perhaps still do. The American Indians and their rain dances are good examples.

How many prayers have been offered by people because of the weather? This is an admission of man that, however smart he may be, he cannot make one drop of rain fall. The Lord is still in control of the weather. And for all of the sophisticated weather equipment and reporting, meteorologists still miss the mark widely sometimes.

In this age with food stacked rows deep on supermarket shelves and weather news coming comfortably into homes via color television sets, it is good for all people to be reminded with Zechariah's people of what verse 1 says. "Ask the LORD for rain in the springtime; it is the LORD who makes the storm clouds. He gives showers of rain to men, and plants of the field to everyone."

From the knowledge of where the weather comes from, it is no accident that the Lord leads into the next topic— idols and false shepherds. These were the ones who took credit for God's action. They spoke their own brand of wisdom, but the Lord called it lies and deceit. It was not enough that the gods were unable to tell anything that was going to happen; they even had to lie too!

The Lord is truth; his Word is the truth; anything apart from him is a lie. As the text says, people who listen to these lies will wander away from the truth: "Therefore the people wander like sheep." They will also experience spiritual wonder. They will ask with Pilate, "What is truth?" Their gods will lead them from one will-o'-the-wisp to another. The prophet Zechariah used the words *deceit, lie, false,* and *vain* in verse 2 for a reason. These are all words that describe the efforts of idols and diviners.

With the picture of sheep and the flock before us, verse 3 directs our attention to the shepherds. The Lord's anger burned against the shepherds. The word here translated for *shepherd* can also be translated "leader." In the context of sheep, this leader is, of course, a shepherd. In the context of people, it is anyone who is in a leading capacity.

The Lord tells us that he is going to be the one to care for the people. We know him from the New Testament as the Good Shepherd (John chapter 10). He wants every shepherd of his people to conform to his own style of shepherding. Verses 2 and 3 show us that the crime of the shepherds was that not only did they not lead their people but they gave them into the hands of their enemies. The Good Shepherd would not do this. But the words describe the hired hand: "When he sees the wolf coming, he abandons the sheep and runs away. Then the wolf attacks the flock and scatters it" (John 10:12).

When the Lord leads his people, even though they are characterized as sheep, they become like a proud horse in battle, the cornerstone, the tent peg, the battle bow, like mighty men trampling the muddy streets in battle. The reason is found at the end of verse 5: "*Because the LORD is with them,* they will fight and overthrow the horsemen."

Johann Altenburg's hymn "O Little Flock, Fear Not the Foe," sings this beautifully:

> Amen, Lord Jesus, grant our prayer;
> Great Captain, now Thine arm make bare,
> Fight for us once again!
> So shall Thy saints and martyrs raise
> A mighty chorus to Thy praise,
> World without end. Amen. (TLH 263:4)

⁶ "I will strengthen the house of Judah
and save the house of Joseph.
I will restore them
because I have compassion on them.
They will be as though
I had not rejected them,
for I am the LORD their God
and I will answer them.
⁷ The Ephraimites will become like mighty men,
and their hearts will be glad as with wine.
Their children will see it and be joyful;
their hearts will rejoice in the LORD.
⁸ I will signal for them
and gather them in.
Surely I will redeem them;
they will be as numerous as before.
⁹ Though I scatter them among the peoples,
yet in distant lands they will remember me.
They and their children will survive,
and they will return.
¹⁰ I will bring them back from Egypt
and gather them from Assyria.
I will bring them to Gilead and Lebanon,
and there will not be room enough for them.
¹¹ They will pass through the sea of trouble;
the surging sea will be subdued
and all the depths of the Nile will dry up.
Assyria's pride will be brought down
and Egypt's scepter will pass away.
¹² I will strengthen them in the LORD
and in his name they will walk,"

declares the LORD.

11 Open your doors, O Lebanon,
so that fire may devour your cedars!
² Wail, O pine tree, for the cedar has fallen;
the stately trees are ruined!
Wail, oaks of Bashan;
the dense forest has been cut down!
³ Listen to the wail of the shepherds;
their rich pastures are destroyed!

**Listen to the roar of the lions;
the lush thicket of the Jordan is ruined!**

When Jesus talked about the hired hand in John chapter 10, he showed that the greatest sin of the hired hand was his lack of compassion. The sheep were just animals to him. At the first threat of danger to himself, he left them to fend for themselves. But the Lord is the Good Shepherd. In verse 6 we read of his compassion for his people. He feels for his people. Golgotha is the ultimate proof of this compassion.

This feeling of compassion cannot be manufactured. When the Lord speaks of his compassion for his people, it is a feeling akin to what a mother feels when she looks at her child. In another place the Word poses this question: "Can a mother forget the baby at her breast?" (Isaiah 49:15). Neither can the Lord forget his children. He feels for them. He is compassionate.

Verses 6 to 12 talk about God's harsh action to his people. He did reject and scatter. He did these things because he could not stand the sin and rebellion of his people. On the other hand, he is compassionate, and he is merciful. These same verses show this too: "I will signal for them and gather them in . . . I will bring them back . . . I will strengthen them." This is sweet gospel. This is why we too can join with the Ephraimites in verse 7: "Their hearts will be glad as with wine. Their children will see it and be joyful; their hearts will rejoice in the Lord."

The final verse of chapter 10 speaks of the Lord's name. God's name is everything that stands for him. He is his name. When Moses asked the Lord's name, he was told that it was "I AM." When God proclaimed his name in Exodus chapter 34, he told of his very essence, he spoke his very name: "The LORD, the LORD, the compassionate and gracious God, slow to anger, abounding in love and faithfulness, maintaining love to thousands, and forgiving wickedness, rebellion and sin. Yet he does not leave the guilty unpunished; he punishes the children and their children for the sin of the fathers to the third and fourth generation" (verses 6,7). God's name is the gospel. God's name is also the law.

This knowledge of God's name determines how we walk in life. "I will strengthen them in the LORD and in his name they will walk."

The oracle that began in verse 1 of chapter 9 now closes in the first three verses of chapter 11. It is a picture painted in natural things—cedars, pine trees, oaks, forest pastures, lions, and thickets. "The heavens declare the glory of God; the skies proclaim the work of his hands," the psalmist said (Psalm 19:1).

Here the creation is called to lament the coming judgment of God. "We know that the whole creation has been groaning as in the pains of childbirth right up to the present time" (Romans 8:22).

Favor and Union—two staffs

⁴This is what the LORD my God says: "Pasture the flock marked for slaughter. ⁵Their buyers slaughter them and go unpunished. Those who sell them say, 'Praise the LORD, I am rich!' Their own shepherds do not spare them. ⁶For I will no longer have pity on the people of the land," declares the LORD. "I will hand everyone over to his neighbor and his king. They will oppress the land, and I will not rescue them from their hands."

⁷So I pastured the flock marked for slaughter, particularly the oppressed of the flock. Then I took two staffs and called one Favor and the other Union, and I pastured the flock. ⁸In one month I got rid of the three shepherds.

The flock detested me, and I grew weary of them ⁹and said, "I will not be your shepherd. Let the dying die, and the perishing perish. Let those who are left eat one another's flesh."

This chapter is a prophecy of the Shepherd, Jesus. There is a symbolic picture and personification in the two staffs, Favor and Union. Those two staffs describe two aspects of the blessings God's ancient people stood to receive under the rule of the Good Shepherd.

This does not mean that parts of the prophecy spoken of here did not find an actual fulfillment in Zechariah's day. (The getting rid of the three shepherds in one month, for instance, or the people's rejecting the ministry of Zechariah.) It does mean that, ultimately, the words found complete fulfillment in the Savior, something that we are struck by in reading the passion story when the narrative time and again states, "This happened so that the Scriptures might be fulfilled."

Verses 4 to 6 talk about the Shepherd's unhappiness with his people. They desired other shepherds instead of him. They even desired those shepherds who were in shepherding just for the money, the kind that said (and perhaps *still* say), "Praise the Lord, I am rich." When the true Prophet and Shepherd is rejected, he at last must say, "Have it your way then. If you are not for me, then you are against me, and you will most certainly bear the consequences." In the text the Lord said, "I will not rescue them from their hands." The desire of those who reject the Shepherd becomes their punishment.

According to Jesus' own words, there are only two kinds of shepherds—good and bad. The thing that is shocking to hear in chapter 11 is that the sheep call the Good Shepherd bad! "The flock detested me." Jesus was the Good Shepherd, but no matter. The stubborn flock screamed, "Crucify! Crucify!" He laid down his life, but they were not impressed.

This detesting grieved Jesus. He wept, "O Jerusalem, Jerusalem, you who kill the prophets and stone those sent to you, how often I have longed to gather your children together, as a hen gathers her chicks under her wings, but you were not willing" (Matthew 23:37). The word the evangelists used to describe Jesus' weeping was not a word that shows merely a trembling lip and perhaps a lone tear stealing down the cheek. They used a word that describes loud and hopeless sobbing.

The time will come when the Good Shepherd will make his final pronouncement: "I will not be your shepherd." This finds its final fulfillment with the awful words on judgment day: "Depart from me, you who are cursed into the eternal fire prepared for the devil and his angels" (Matthew 25:41). Finally the time comes when the Lord will break the two staffs, Favor and Union.

We sing, "What a friend we have in Jesus." We admit this with this hymn text: "You treat no other friend so ill" [TLH 650:1] God wants to be our friend; he wanted to be the friend of Zechariah's people. From young to old, friendship means a great deal. The Lord God wanted to shepherd his people with the staff called Favor! He wanted to be their friend.

Union too. Union—unity—is so important in life. "How good and pleasant it is when brothers live together in unity! (Psalm 133:1). How much better this unity is when it exists between God and his people. This unity doesn't exist because God has lowered his requirements for righteousness. Rather, it comes only because God the Father has made a way through his Son, Jesus, whereby all people can truly be united with him.

We cannot be sure who the three shepherds were who were gotten rid of in three months (verse 8). They were some threat to the flock. The shepherds, here the prophet and, in the wider prophecy, Jesus himself, have acted like good shepherds. They have gotten rid of the threat. But this action went unappreciated. The flock detested the shepherds—even shepherds with the flock's best interest at heart. The sheep turned on their own shepherds!

It is a small wonder why the shepherd finally admitted, "I grew weary of them." Centuries earlier Pharaoh had insisted on hardening his heart. Finally, the God of infinite patience said, "Be hard, then." And the heart of stone sank that way in the Red Sea. "Let the dying die and the perishing perish." This is the frightful but inevitable result of detesting the Shepherd.

¹⁰Then I took my staff called Favor and broke it, revoking the covenant I had made with all the nations. ¹¹It was revoked on that day, and so the afflicted of the flock who were watching me knew it was the word of the LORD.

¹²I told them, "If you think it best, give me my pay; but if not, keep it." So they paid me thirty pieces of silver.

¹³And the LORD said to me, "Throw it to the potter"—the handsome price at which they priced me! So I took the thirty pieces of silver and threw them into the house of the LORD to the potter.

¹⁴Then I broke my second staff called Union, breaking the brotherhood between Judah and Israel.

Finally the staff called Favor is broken, symbolizing that God would withdraw his gracious offer. "How long, O Lord?" is what the saints cry in heaven. That cry is twofold. "How long until you save your people? How long until you bring to justice those who have snubbed you?"

The covenant is finally revoked with the unwilling. They were the ones who really abrogated it. And on that day when God's patience finally runs out against the unbelief of this world it will be equally true: "The afflicted of the flock who were watching me knew it was the word of the LORD." Just as Noah and his family heard the muffled cries outside the ark and the hammerblows of the storm, they too knew that the awful act of judgment was the Word of the Lord, who will not permit his gracious offer to be trampled underfoot.

The incredible thing is how cheaply the world values their shepherds. How much is a faithful pastor worth? (Remember that the word *pastor* means "shepherd" and that the prototype of all pastors is Jesus.) The world does not place a high premium on the work of godly ministers, on the shepherding of souls. Jesus, the Good Shepherd, was only worth 30 pieces of silver. Judas would not have gotten rich on the money had he kept it. The potter's field was not choice real estate around Jerusalem. It remained a monument to what the world thought of shepherds in general and the Shepherd in particular.

Zechariah's people paid more for the care of their bodies than they thought they needed to pay for the care of their souls. Naaman, the leper, came to be healed in his body with 750 pounds of silver and 150 pounds of gold (2 Kings 5:5). But salvation and healing of the soul—well, 30 pieces of silver will do for that!

It was an insult to the blood of the Lamb. The work of the Shepherd was free. Salvation is free, but it is not cheap. It was accomplished not with 30 pieces of dirty silver but with his holy precious blood and innocent suffering and death.

The Lord's words through the prophet drip with sarcasm: "The handsome price at which they priced me."

Verse 14 tells us that the staff called Union was also broken.

True union, whether between Judah and Israel or between any two parties, depends on their belief in God. Where there is no agreement on how we believe in the triune God, there can be no true union. How can there be when the very most important thing in life is left in question? This holds true in the church. It also holds true in the state and even in marriage. It holds true between all people in whatever situation they are in. This fact remains: "What harmony is there between Christ and Belial? What does a believer have in common with an unbeliever?" (2 Corinthians 6:15).

¹⁵**Then the Lord said to me, "Take again the equipment of a foolish shepherd. ¹⁶For I am going to raise up a shepherd over the land who will not care for the lost, or seek the young, or heal the injured, or feed the healthy, but will eat the meat of the choice sheep, tearing off their hoofs.**

¹⁷ **"Woe to the worthless shepherd,**
     who deserts the flock!
May the sword strike his arm and his right eye!
     May his arm be completely withered,
     his right eye totally blinded!"

"You do not want the Good Shepherd? Then have a bad shepherd." This was God's verdict.

This bad shepherd would not do all of the things a good shepherd does. The list provides a very good summary of the work a good shepherd does: (1) he goes looking for the lost, (2) he seeks the young, both the young in years and the young in faith, (3) he works to heal those who have gotten hurt in their faith (in the spirit of Galatians 6:1: "Brothers, if someone is caught in a sin, you who are spiritual should restore him gently"), and (4) he works continually to provide for the needs of the healthy that they might remain healthy. In the case of the bad shepherd, he does the opposite of all these things a good shepherd would do.

The closing verse of the chapter contains the final woe. There is judgment spoken of here both to the flock and to the shepherd—to the flock because it detested the Good Shepherd, and to the shepherd because he failed in his sacred duties of shepherding. Such a bad shepherd, according to the description of this verse, was to end his existence crippled. The eyes, hands, and abilities he used to exploit and rob were to be taken from him. As in the case of the stewards in the New Testament parable, the unfaithful will have even what they had taken away from them.

Jerusalem's enemies to be destroyed

An Oracle

12 This is the word of the LORD concerning Israel. The LORD, who stretches out the heavens, who lays the foundation of the earth, and who forms the spirit of man within him, declares: ²"I am going to make Jerusalem a cup that sends all the surrounding peoples reeling. Judah will be besieged as well as Jerusalem. ³On that day, when all the nations of the earth are gathered against her, I will make Jerusalem an immovable rock for all the nations. All who try to move it will injure themselves. ⁴On that day I will strike every horse with panic and its rider with madness," declares the LORD. "I will keep a watchful eye over the house of Judah, but I will blind all the horses of the nations. ⁵Then the leaders of Judah will say in their hearts, 'The people of Jerusalem are strong, because the LORD Almighty is their God.'

⁶"On that day I will make the leaders of Judah like a firepot in a woodpile, like a flaming torch among sheaves. They will consume right and left all the surrounding peoples, but Jerusalem will remain intact in her place.

⁷"The LORD will save the dwellings of Judah first, so that the honor of the house of David and of Jerusalem's inhabitants may not be greater than that of Judah. ⁸On that day the LORD will shield those who live in Jerusalem, so that the feeblest among them will be like David, and the house of David will be like God, like the Angel of the LORD going before them. ⁹On that day I will set out to destroy all the nations that attack Jerusalem.

This chapter begins another section of prophecy in which Zechariah describes what the Lord was going to do for the Israelites. This prophecy continues through to the end of the book. The people around the Israelites were also mentioned in this prophecy because they were involved in the promises. Unfortunately for the nations around God's people, what was good news for Judah would be bad news for them.

In verses 1 to 5 the Lord goes back to the beginning, to creation. When he spoke to establish his credentials as deliverer and preserver, what better example than to point to the beginning. If he was able to stretch out the heavens above the earth, lay the foundations of this world on the face of the deep, and form the spirit of the man, then can he not also take care of problems and present dangers?

The problems of God's people seemed big until they were placed into their proper perspective. The God of creation could easily take care of them.

It was not that the people would escape with no problems. Verses 2 to 4 speak about trouble and hard times, about siege and battle. Jesus prayed to his Father for all disciples: "My prayer is not that you take them out of the world but that you protect them from the evil one" (John 17:15). And God's people do continue to stand as was the promise to Zechariah's people, an immovable rock for all the nations.

> Built on the Rock the church shall stand
> Even when steeples are falling.
> Crumbled have spires in ev'ry land;
> Bells still are chiming and calling,
> Calling the young and old to rest,
> But above all the soul distressed,
> Longing for rest everlasting. (CW 529:1)

The Lord worked his protection in two ways. He promised first to make his people impregnable. They were to be like a rock that no one could move. If the enemy tried to destroy them, they would just bloody their hands and break their backs. God also promised to make the enemy unable to fight. He would strike the horse and rider with panic and madness. These were, indeed, God's ways. Many examples of this stand in Scripture, one being Midian's conflict against Gideon. When the Midianites invaded Israel's homeland, God turned the swords of the enemy against themselves (Judges 7).

Verse 5 clinches the safety of God's people. They were strong when God was with them and because their God was with them. With God they were strong; without God they were weak. The history of God's people is a story of these two extremes, of the ceaseless vacillation between the two poles of strength and weakness. It is the story of our own lives too. Our weakness becomes overpowering when we drift away from the source of our strength. But our weakness becomes strength when we remain with God. "When I am weak, then I am strong," the apostle was able to say (2 Corinthians 12:10).

Verses 6 to 9 continue the theme of deliverance. The Lord became eloquent. He made sweeping promises of help and deliverance. As he talked, it almost seems that he got carried away with his power and with his promise.

Verse 6 describes overwhelming power. A woodpile is no match for a fire. A pile of sheaves offers no resistance to a torch. The fire in both cases is going to have easy work of it. It is even in the nature of fuel to succumb to the fire. This is the comparison God makes about the ultimate outcome between good and bad, between his people and the people who come against his people.

To magnify his miracle, God promised to save what by itself was feeble (verses 7-9). The Lord made a point of saving the tents of Judah before he saved the walled city of Jerusalem. In verse 8 he talked about the feeblest—the one who could not stand by himself. The word for feeble here is a word that means "to stagger or stumble." Jonathan's lame son, Mephibosheth, when he was shown kindness by David, said, "What is your servant, that you should notice a dead dog like me?" (2 Samuel 9:8). Now the picture of strength and capability goes from the likes of Mephibosheth to David and from David to God himself. What an acceleration of strength!

The final picture is the picture of the Angel of the Lord going on before the people. The Angel of the Lord is elsewhere equated with Jesus himself, God made flesh. This is God in visible human form who goes before his people and fights for them as the hymn writer said:

> Amen, Lord Jesus, grant our prayer;
> Great Captain, now Thine arm make bare,
> Fight for us once again!
> So shall Thy saints and martyrs raise
> A mighty chorus to Thy praise,
> World without end. Amen. (TLH 263:4)

Divine retribution! Vengeance is God's; he will repay. "I will set out to destroy all the nations that attack Jerusalem."

Mourning for the one they pierced

¹⁰"And I will pour out on the house of David and the inhabitants of Jerusalem a spirit of grace and supplication. They will look on me, the one they have pierced, and they will mourn for him as one mourns for an only child, and grieve bitterly for him as one grieves for a firstborn son. ¹¹On that day the weeping in Jerusalem will be great, like the weeping of Hadad Rimmon in the plain of Megiddo. ¹²The land will mourn, each clan by itself, with their wives by themselves: the clan of the house of David and their wives, the clan of the house of Nathan and their wives, ¹³the clan of the house of Levi and their wives, the clan of Shimei and their wives, ¹⁴and all the rest of the clans and their wives."

There is some uncertainty as to whether the spirit in verse 10 refers to the Holy Spirit or whether it is a spirit given to the people, a motivating spirit or attitude. It could be both. It is this in Psalm 51:10,11: "Create in me a pure heart, O God, and renew a *steadfast spirit* within me. Do not cast me from your presence or take your *Holy Spirit* from me."

The spirit of verse 10 is associated with grace and supplication. These two attributes certainly speak of God's Holy Spirit. The word in Hebrew, here translated *grace,* is a word that also means "charm" or "favor."

Romans chapter 8 makes the connection that when we talk about the Holy Spirit, we are also talking about the spirit we have as a result of his working. "The mind controlled by the Spirit is life and peace" (verse 6). God's favor rests upon us when we are privileged to call him Father: "You received the Spirit of sonship. And by him we cry, '*Abba,* Father'" (verse 15). And verses 26 and 27 speak about the favor and grace we enjoy as the result of the Spirit's intercession for us: "The Spirit helps us in our weakness. We do not know what we ought to pray for, but the Spirit himself intercedes for us with groans that words cannot express. . . . The Spirit intercedes for the saints in accordance with God's will."

It is also the work of the Holy Spirit that God's people are led to repentance. In David's words of repentance for his sin with Bathsheba in Psalm 51, he mentioned God's Spirit several times: "Do not . . . take your Holy Spirit from me" (verse 11). And Ananias and Sapphira, who did not repent of their sin of lying, were told by Peter, "You have lied to the Holy Spirit. . . . How could you agree to test the Spirit of the Lord?" (Acts 5:3,9).

Repentance brought through God's Spirit brings weeping with it, a weeping of sorrow and loss and deprivation. The Lutheran Confessions describe contrition as "terror smiting the conscience over a knowledge of sin." Someone has died. Someone *must* die. We are guilty. Zechariah's people were drawn with all people to the foot of the cross where they too saw the one they pierced.

We learn from 2 Chronicles 35:20-24 that it was on the plains of Megiddo that good King Josiah was shot and killed by archers of Egypt's Pharaoh Neco. Verse 24 says, "He was buried in the tombs of his fathers, and all Judah and Jerusalem mourned for him." The mourning described by Zechariah is like the mourning for an only child, for a first born, for a good king.

The horrifying thing is that we do not feel more grief for what we have done. We, with Zechariah's people, killed God's Son! Yet when this message is preached in churches, people fidget, yawn, and look furtively at their watches, ,slipped secretly from the sleeves of their suitcoats.

This awful apathy was also felt by the hymn writer who confessed:

> Thus might I hide my blushing face
> While his dear cross appears,
> Dissolve my heart in thankfulness,
> And melt my eyes to tears. (CW 129:4)

To this we too join, "Lord dissolve my heart, and melt my eyes to tears." By ourselves this kind of sorrow is not going to happen. We desire this Spirit of grace and supplication that will lead us to godly sorrow over our sins. Forgive us, forgiving Spirit, for our dry eyes.

Verses 12 and 13 list the clans, families, wives, and children—everyone! This was not political mourning, with its entourage of respectable representative mourners. The grief would sweep over everyone—fathers, mothers, boys, and girls. All have reason to weep as they struggle up the slopes of Golgotha to behold the one *they* pierced.

Cleansing from sin

13 "On that day a fountain will be opened to the house of David and the inhabitants of Jerusalem, to cleanse them from sin and impurity.

²"On that day, I will banish the names of the idols from the land, and they will be remembered no more," declares the LORD Almighty. "I will remove both the prophets and the spirit of impurity from the land. ³And if anyone still prophesies, his father and mother, to whom he was born, will say to him, 'You must die, because you have told lies in the LORD's name.' When he prophesies, his own parents will stab him.

⁴"On that day every prophet will be ashamed of his prophetic vision. He will not put on a prophet's garment of hair in order to deceive. ⁵He will say, 'I am not a prophet. I am a farmer; the land has been my livelihood since my youth.' ⁶If someone asks him, 'What are these wounds on your body?' he will answer, 'The wounds I was given at the house of my friends.'"

In 1771 William Cowper penned this hymn verse:

> There is a fountain filled with blood—
> Immanuel was slain—
> And sinners who are washed there-in
> Lose ev'ry guilty stain. (CW 112:1)

Cowper used verse 1 as his inspiration. The chapter goes on to describe how the Lord would rid the land of false religion—on that day. We speak wistfully of the day, of *the* day. That will be the day! we say, when our church is no longer plagued by evil and by falsehood, when the devil does not steal away our members and turn them into strangers who confess some foreign religious idea.

When the Lord speaks about that day, we, of course, are not given a definite year, month, or day. We do see, as we see in all prophecy, different steps in the fulfillment. As the end of the world is shown in Matthew chapters 24 and 25— some of the events already fulfilled—so it is in Zechariah's prophecy. Certainly there were times in Israel's history when the evil prophets were driven out. There were days of spiritual housecleaning.

In fact, the history of God's people is one long repetition of the fact that they rid themselves of the evil through the judges and prophets only to find themselves at a later day with the evil once more entrenched in the form of false religion.

The Reformation would be a day when, to a certain degree, the evil was removed, the prophets and the spirit of impurity from the land.

Martin Luther wrote in one of his hymns, "O God, root out all heresy, and of false teachers rid us" (CW 205:2). As heirs of the Reformation, you and I live in an era when the good news of full and free forgiveness in Christ is preached widely.

The final day of cleansing will be the day of judgment. Revelation 20:10 foretells it: "The devil, who deceived them, was thrown into the lake of burning sulfur, where the beast and the false prophet had been thrown. They will be tormented day and night for ever and ever." Notice that this prophecy, which lies in the future, is written as if it is already accomplished! It is as good as done! Zechariah, the prophet of God, has spoken; it will happen.

God's truth will stand. Verse 3 points out that even the closest ties of human beings—those between parents, mother and father—will be abandoned if they get in the way of truth. Parents will not even stand up for their own children if these children stand as a threat to the truth. The false prophet will be forced to seek other employment, something completely different from his evil trade—like farming. Verse 6 ties in with verse 3. Friends will even rise up against friends and wound them if they see them tampering with God's truth.

What a good day it will be when the Lord finally calls an end to all false religion! The saints in heaven are crying, "How long?" And we join their cry.

The Shepherd struck, the sheep scattered

> [7] "Awake, O sword, against my shepherd,
>   against the man who is close to me!"
>   declares the LORD Almighty.
> "Strike the shepherd,
>   and the sheep will be scattered,
>   and I will turn my hand against the little ones.
> [8] In the whole land," declares the LORD,
>   "two-thirds will be struck down and perish;
>   yet one-third will be left in it.
> [9] This third I will bring into the fire;
>   I will refine them like silver
>   and test them like gold.
> They will call on my name
>   and I will answer them;
> I will say, 'They are my people,'
>   and they will say, 'The LORD is our God.'"

The Lord Almighty spoke these words. He is God the Father. The section has quotation marks around it.

The shepherd mentioned is none other than Jesus himself, the Good Shepherd. Jesus quoted these words on the night of his death (Mark 14:27). He knew as he sat with his disciples at the Last Supper that the sword of the prophet Zechariah was soon to strike him down. He knew also that the sheep would be scattered to the night wind of Gethsemane as it wafted its chill through Jerusalem and even down the road to Emmaus, "We had hoped that he was the one who was going to redeem Israel" (Luke 24:21).

Verses 8 and 9 speak of refining from the throngs on Palm Sunday to the handful of people on Maundy Thursday to the forlorn little groups on Easter Sunday. It was a time of refining "in the whole land," as verse 8 described it. The church was different. The disciples, who before Jesus' death feared persecution, welcomed suffering for their faith. When they were beaten, they rejoiced "because they had been counted worthy of suffering disgrace for the Name" (Acts 5:41). This was gold that had been purified. They knew the Name. They called on it as Zechariah had foretold. They gladly suffered for it.

God's purification is not a destructive process but a constructive process. The outcome is that we say, "The Lord is our God," and he in turn now looks at us with our dross to consume and our gold to refine and says, "These are my people."

Purification is achieved through fire. The fires of life simply teach us more and more to say, "The Lord is my God. Only he can save me through this fire. The Lord is my God. Only he can be so concerned about the good and bad in me. The Lord is my God. He wants to do this so that I become more and more like him in thought and being. The Lord is my God. How can I be impure if the Lord is my God? How can I think of trying to escape the fire of purification if the Lord is my God?" And when faith grows weak and flickers dimly on the walls of our hearts, we say, "The Lord is my God!" When death comes, and we step into that lonely valley of the shadow, we will say, "The Lord is my God!"

The outcome of the fire is that God's people are pure, safe, and valuable forever. Because Jesus was stricken, we are different. We have the cross, and it makes a difference. What would our church be without this cross, this symbol that the Father did indeed put the sword to his own Son's life in order to make a way to save ours. Through the awful sacrifice of the Shepherd, the Father now says, "These are my people."

The Lord comes and reigns

14 A day of the LORD is coming when your plunder will be divided among you.

²I will gather all the nations to Jerusalem to fight against it; the city will be captured, the houses ransacked, and the women raped. Half of the city will go into exile, but the rest of the people will not be taken from the city.

³Then the LORD will go out and fight against those nations, as he fights in the day of battle. ⁴On that day his feet will stand on the Mount of Olives, east of Jerusalem, and the Mount of Olives will be split in two from east to west, forming a great valley, with half of the mountain moving north and half moving south. ⁵You will flee by my mountain valley, for it will extend to Azel. You will flee as you fled from the earthquake in the days of Uzziah king of Judah. Then the LORD my God will come, and all the holy ones with him.

⁶On that day there will be no light, no cold or frost. ⁷It will be a unique day, without daytime or nighttime—a day know to the LORD. When evening comes, there will be light.

This last chapter of Zechariah is prophecy that falls into the same description that previous prophecy has fallen. (See comments on 13:1.)

It is obvious that the Lord is speaking figuratively in this last chapter when he speaks of mountains splitting, of days without light, of time with no cold or frost, when the normal course of nature is reversed with light coming at evening, of living water, and of bells on horses and cooking pots. The prophetic pot of these verses is seasoned with familiar seasonings to give us a flavor of what is coming: *the great day!*

During Israel's long history the Lord often used surrounding nations to punish his people. After these nations punished his people, he in turn punished the nations. This is a pattern that he established, and it is a pattern that extends into the future. After the evils of siege and destruction and the evils that warfare brings with it (plundering and rape), there follows the great reversal when the Lord turns and defends his people.

The descriptions given here do not fit any particular historical event; the phrase "half of the city" shows this because we know of no historical exile in which half of the people were taken and half left. But the fact is clear from these verses that, whatever evil would overtake God's people, he was going to fight for them. Thunder accompanied his approach, the kind that made the mountains shake. This was the way he came to rescue. It happened at Mount Sinai (Exodus 19:16). The Lord spoke through the prophet Isaiah, "Though the mountains be shaken and the hills be removed, yet my unfailing love for you will not be shaken" (Isaiah 54:10). John the Baptists, the great forerunner of Jesus, proclaimed, "Every valley shall be filled in, every mountain and hill made low" (Luke 3:4). And Zechariah, in these verses, spoke about the mountains being split and about resulting valleys of safety and escape.

Jesus is coming, and Zechariah was right: "Then the LORD my God will come, and all the holy ones with him." "We believe that Jesus died and rose again and so we believe that God will bring with Jesus those who have fallen asleep in him" (1 Thessalonians 4:14).

On that day!

⁸**On that day living water will flow out from Jerusalem, half to the eastern sea and half to the western sea, in summer and in winter.**

⁹**The LORD will be king over the whole earth. On that day there will be one LORD, and his name the only name.**

¹⁰**The whole land, from Geba to Rimmon, south of Jerusalem, will become like the Arabah. But Jerusalem will be raised up and remain in its place, from the Benjamin Gate to the site of the**

First Gate, to the Corner Gate, and from the Tower of Hananel to the royal winepresses. ¹¹It will be inhabited; never again will it be destroyed. Jerusalem will be secure.

The striking thing about these verses is the parallel they have in New Testament revelation about the coming of Jesus and his new Jerusalem. Zechariah said it is a day known to the Lord. Jesus himself said, "No one knows about that day or hour, not even the angels in heaven, nor the Son, but only the Father" (Matthew 24:36).

Zechariah said, "It will be a unique day, without daytime or nighttime—when evening comes, there will be light." The apostle John said, "The city does not need the sun or the moon to shine on it, for the glory of God gives it light, and the Lamb is its lamp. The nations will walk by its light, and the kings of the earth will bring their splendor into it. On no day will its gates ever be shut, for there will be no night there" (Revelation 21:23-25). Zechariah said, "On that day living water will flow out from Jerusalem." The book of Revelation also says, "Then the angel showed me the river of the water of life, as clear as crystal, flowing from the throne of God and of the Lamb down the middle of the great street of the city" (22:1,2). Zechariah said, "The Lord will be king over the whole earth. On that day there will be one Lord, and his name the only name." The apostle Paul said, "Therefore God exalted him to the highest place and gave him the name that is above every name, that at the name of Jesus every knee should bow, in heaven and on earth and under the earth, and every tongue confess that Jesus Christ is Lord, to the glory of God the Father" (Philippians 2:9-11).

Zechariah spoke about everything but Jerusalem being destroyed and becoming like the desert wasteland to the south of the Dead Sea, the Arabah. Peter said, "The day of the Lord will come like a thief. The heavens will disappear with a roar; the elements will be destroyed by fire, and the earth and everything in it will be laid bare" (2 Peter 3:10).

What a wonderful testimony these comparisons of prophecy are! How well they describe this day of the Lord that is most certainly coming and that has been so clear in the prophets' eyes for so long. The apostle Peter's further words to his people are certainly fitting for us to hear too: "Since everything will be destroyed in this way, what kind of people ought you to be? You ought to live holy and godly lives as you look forward to the day of God and speed its coming" (2 Peter 3:11,12).

On that day!

The Lord comes and reigns

¹²This is the plague with which the LORD will strike all the nations that fought against Jerusalem: Their flesh will rot while they are still standing on their feet, their eyes will rot in their sockets, and their tongues will rot in their mouths. ¹³On that day men will be stricken by the LORD with great panic. Each man will seize the hand of another, and they will attack each other. ¹⁴Judah too will fight at Jerusalem. The wealth of all the surrounding nations will be collected—great quantities of gold and silver and clothing. ¹⁵A similar plague will strike the horses and mules, the camels and donkeys, and all the animals in those camps.

¹⁶Then the survivors from all the nations that have attacked Jerusalem will go up year after year to worship the King, the LORD Almighty, and to celebrate the Feast of Tabernacles. ¹⁷If any of the peoples of the earth do not go up to Jerusalem to worship the King, the LORD Almighty, they will have no rain. ¹⁸If the Egyptian people do not go up and take part, they will have no rain. The LORD will bring on them the plague he inflicts on the nations that do not go up to celebrate the Feast of Tabernacles. ¹⁹This will be the punishment of Egypt and the punishment of all the nations that do not go up to celebrate the Feast of Tabernacles.

²⁰On that day HOLY TO THE LORD will be inscribed on the bells of the horses, and the cooking pots in the LORD's house will

be like the sacred bowls in front of the altar. ²¹Every pot in Jerusalem and Judah will be holy to the LORD Almighty, and all who come to sacrifice will take some of the pots and cook in them. And on that day there will no longer be a Canaanite in the house of the LORD Almighty.

The plague to strike against the enemies of God's people will completely disfigure and destroy. This leprosy of punishment will quickly devour the skin. People unclean by their actions will have no choice but to shout out, "Unclean! Unclean!" when their flesh rots. It is a gruesome fact of life to those without Jesus and to those against Jesus. Job's hope was, "After my skin has been destroyed, yet in my flesh I will see God" (19:26). When God's judgment strikes, eyes will be destroyed; tongues will be destroyed. After they are gone, there will be no more chance to see or speak. What a complete and awful punishment! Verse 15 even includes the animals in the plagues. The whole creation is affected and infected.

The panic of verse 13 is also echoed in the book of Revelation: "The agony they suffered was like that of the sting of a scorpion when it strikes a man. During those days men will seek death, but will not find it; they will long to die, but death will elude them" (9:5,6). On that day!

God's people plundered the Egyptians when they made their exodus from the land of slavery. To the victor belongs the spoils! It was true. The wealth of surrounding nations will be collected. The promise is that God's people will be sitting on thrones ruling; all things will be theirs. This is a promise from the one who has power to carry it out and whose good pleasure it is to do it.

No rain! What a curse it is to see all things dry up and die and to be helpless to do anything about it. This was the final curse that would and will strike all those who do not worship the true God. Apart from him there is no life.

The Feast of Tabernacles was also known as the Feast of Ingathering. It was a harvest festival established by the Lord in Leviticus chapter 23, beginning with verse 33. At the end of the regulations for that feast we read, "Live in booths for seven days . . . so your descendants will know that I had the Israelites live in booths *when I brought them out of Egypt*" (verses 42,43). The very people who provided the background for this feast—the Egyptians—were going to be cursed if they did not participate!

Bring the firstfruits to the Lord! That is what the feast required. Curses followed otherwise. The Lord clearly said through the prophet Malachi, "You are under a curse—the whole nation of you—because you are robbing me. Bring the whole tithe into the storehouse, that there may be food in my house" (3:9,10).

Verses 20 and 21 are the final verses of the book of Zechariah. At first glance they may seem anticlimactic, even disappointing in the apparent importance of their parting thoughts. But consider the wonderful hope they offer. The inscription found on the high priest's turban, HOLY TO THE LORD, will be inscribed on everything, down to the bells on the horses and the cooking pots! In other words, for believers living in the New Testament era, there is no distinction between sacred and secular. The Lord's people dedicate all of their resources to the service of God.

Everyone will realize on the great day of the Lord that everything exists only for the Lord. They are there to praise only him forever and to be completely happy in doing this. The First Commandment, which asks us to recognize him as the only reason for our existence and for our praise, will finally be kept perfectly. We will love the Lord our God with all our hearts and with all our souls and with all our minds. Every single thought, action, word, and thing will be stamped HOLY TO THE LORD. No one will be foreign to that idea or against it. Finally, in heaven there will be no Canaanite in the house, no one outside God's family, as verse 21 promises.

Yes, this is the grandest of promises and aspirations! This is the way it will be—on that day!

I Will Send My Messenger
(1:1–4:5)

Jacob loved; Esau hated

1 An oracle: The word of the LORD to Israel through Malachi.

²"I have loved you," says the LORD.
"But you ask, 'How have you loved us?'
"Was not Esau Jacob's brother?" the LORD says. "Yet I have loved Jacob, ³but Esau I have hated, and I have turned his mountains into a wasteland and left his inheritance to the desert jackals."

⁴Edom may say, "Though we have been crushed, we will rebuild the ruins."

But this is what the LORD Almighty says: "They may build, but I will demolish. They will be called the Wicked Land, a people always under the wrath of the LORD. ⁵You will see it with your own eyes and say, 'Great is the LORD—even beyond the borders of Israel!'"

We know nothing about the prophet Malachi apart from what we learn of him from this book. He, no doubt, was a contemporary of the prophet Nehemiah four centuries before Christ was born. The conditions described in both books seem to parallel each other. It also seems that from references to God's house in 1:6 and 3:10, the temple was rebuilt at the time he wrote his book. His was to be the last word of recorded prophecy for four hundred years, until the coming of the Lord.

The first verse calls what follows an oracle. The word *oracle* is the translation of the very first word in the Hebrew text of the book of Malachi. The word actually comes from the word meaning "to carry something" and is in other places translated "burden."

The idea of a burden is right and good. When God comes to his messenger—which is what the name Malachi means—he places a burden on him, a burden of words that he must take to the people. Jeremiah felt this burden. He said, "If I say, 'I will not mention him or speak any more in his name,' his word is in my heart like a fire, a fire shut up in my bones. I am weary of holding it in; indeed, I cannot" (Jeremiah 20:9). The apostle Paul also felt this burden of being the Lord's messenger when he said, "When I preach the gospel, I cannot boast, for I am compelled to preach. Woe to me if I do not preach the gospel!" (1 Corinthians 9:16).

There are many so-called messengers (angels) who flutter down on the scene in their own employ and at their own bidding with some "burden," some message they feel constrained to deliver. But only the Lord's messengers carry a true message. The false prophets realize this: "You must not mention 'the oracle of the LORD' again, because every man's own word becomes his oracle and so you distort the words of the living God, the LORD Almighty, our God" (Jeremiah 23:36). In that chapter of Jeremiah, the Lord is talking about lying prophets.

What follows in the book of Malachi is the true oracle—burden—of God given to Malachi, his messenger.

Verses 2 to 6 talk about God's love. That is to be the emphasis. "I have loved you." That is what the Lord spoke in preview of John 3:16. The topic before us is love, God's love.

We need to keep in mind the Lord's love for his people, because it is easy to get sidetracked on his harsh treatment of Esau and forget that he acted and dealt in love to his people even when he said about Esau, "They will be called The Wicked Land, a people always under the wrath of the LORD."

In Psalm 52 David talked to God about Doeg the Edomite, one of Esau's descendants. Doeg was the one who went to Saul and told him about David's going to Ahimelech, and David said about him, "Surely God will bring you down to everlasting ruin: He will snatch you up and tear you from your tent; he will uproot you from the land of the living" (verse 5). The point of mentioning this is that God's protection of his people stems from his love for them. From the enemies' viewpoint, we see only the retribution and anger; with God's people in sight, we see the love.

The Lord calls his protection love. But the people of Malachi's day questioned this, and so do people today. "How have you loved us?" we all ask. The question can be rephrased: "What have you ever done for us?" God's love appears elusive and hidden, especially when times are hard. The question springs to our lips: "How can a loving God do such things?" There usually is indignation in the voice of the one asking the question, as if God is somehow betraying his creation.

The fact is that if God is really true and right, he *must* hate evil and he *must* hate people who do evil. How can he do anything but punish the evil and banish it forever from himself? This is the curse; this is hell. This is necessary if God is really what we hope he is—the epitome and champion of right and good.

The record stands: "[God] wants all men to be saved and to come to a knowledge of the truth" (1 Timothy

127

2:4). There is also the fact that some reject this desire of God to save them—people like Edom in chapter 1 of Malachi. The sin is recorded in Numbers chapter 20. Moses there pleaded for passage through the country of Edom as the Israelites made their way back home from the bondage of Egypt. They even volunteered to pay, and they began their request with these words: "This is what your brother Israel says" (verse 14). But Edom refused: "You may not pass through here; if you try, we will march out and attack you with the sword" (verse 18). And they meant what they said: "Then Edom came out against them with a large and powerful army" (verse 20). Psalm 137:7 also states, "Remember, O LORD, what the Edomites did on the day Jerusalem fell. 'Tear it down,' they cried, 'tear it down to its foundations!' "

There are only two positions in which life is lived: for God or against God. Those for him have his unfailing love and protection. Those against him have his unfailing hatred and destruction. In the words before us, this situation is summed up: "I have loved Jacob, but Esau I have hated." The word *hated* is a strong word. To people who complained, "God doesn't care about us," Malachi was saying, "Why, you're the recipients of *special love*, love God withheld from Esau."

It is truly "a dreadful thing to fall into the hands of the living God" (Hebrews 10:31). Life goes bad, like Pharaoh's chariot without wheels. Gamaliel, in the book of Acts, had it right—and Edom experienced it: "If it is from God, you will not be able to stop these men; you will only find yourselves fighting against God" (Acts 5:39). And God always wins.

On God's side or against him—beloved or hated—these are the only choices.

You sacrifice crippled or diseased animals

Blemished sacrifices

⁶"A son honors his father, and a servant his master. If I am a father, where is the honor due me? If I am a master, where is the respect due me?" says the LORD Almighty. "It is you, O priests, who show contempt for my name.

"But you ask, 'How have we shown contempt for your name?'

⁷"You place defiled food on my altar.

"But you ask, 'How have we defiled you?'

"By saying that the LORD's table is contemptible. ⁸When you bring blind animals for sacrifice, is that not wrong? When you sacrifice crippled or diseased animals, is that not wrong? Try offering them to your governor! Would he be pleased with you? Would he accept you?" says the LORD Almighty.

⁹"Now implore God to be gracious to us. With such offerings from your hands, will he accept you?"—says the LORD Almighty.

¹⁰"Oh, that one of you would shut the temple doors, so that you would not light useless fires on my altar! I am not pleased with you," says the LORD Almighty, "and I will accept no offering from your hands. ¹¹My name will be great among the nations, from the rising to the setting of the sun. In every place incense and pure offerings will be brought to my name, because my name will be great among the nations," says the LORD Almighty.

¹²"But you profane it by saying of the Lord's table, 'It is defiled,' and of its food, 'It is contemptible.' ¹³And you say, 'What a burden!' and you sniff at it contemptuously," says the LORD Almighty.

"When you bring injured, crippled or diseased animals and offer them as sacrifices, should I accept them from your hands?" says the LORD. ¹⁴"Cursed is the cheat who has an acceptable male in his flock and vows to give it, but then sacrifices a blemished animal to the Lord. For I am a great king," says the LORD Almighty, "and my name is to be feared among the nations."

The Lord looked at the offerings of his people. He wanted them to know that these offerings were important to him.

This section of the Bible had to be written because of our human nature. When the Jews went to their flocks to pick out the sacrifice for God, God was very quiet. He was

so quiet, and apparently unknowing, that the person looking for a good sheep could very well reason to himself:
"The Lord made everything and owns everything anyway.
What difference does it make what I give him or *if* I give
him anything at all?"

The struggle to give something good was losing out, and
the offerings were limping (apparently literally!). It seemed
right to give something. It wasn't that the people were not
giving. They were bringing the Lord offerings, all right, but
their gifts were not acceptable.

In Exodus 23:19 God had instructed his people, "Bring
the best of the firstfruits of your soil to the house of the LORD
your God." The people also knew the story of Cain and Abel
and their sacrifices to God. Abel's sacrifice was accepted, not
because the Lord liked lambs better than vegetables—Abel
being a shepherd and Cain a farmer—but because "Abel
brought fat portions from some of the firstborn of his flock"
(Genesis 4:4).

What took place at the beginning of the Old Testament
was what was happening at the end of the Old Testament
among Malachi's people. God asked these questions: "If I
am a father, where is the honor due me? If I am a master,
where is the respect due me?" He even said, "Try offering
them [the sacrifices] to your governor! Would he be pleased
with you?"

We have the example in these verses of the dialogue for
which the book of Malachi is characterized. There is talk back
and forth. We can even say there is backtalk. In verse 6 God
says, "It is you, O priests, who show contempt for my name.
But you ask, 'How have we shown contempt for your
name?'" None of God's people knowingly desired a shouting
match with God. But because of their actions, they ended up
that way.

This cheeky disrespect is evidenced in three ways. The first is that the children were not honoring their father. The Fourth Commandment dictates respect and honor to fathers. The Lord, who has taught us to pray "our Father," asked Malachi's people, "If I am a father, where is the honor due me?" The second example of disrespect concerned that between servant and master. The apostle Paul called himself the servant of God—even his slave! Hebrews 9:14 says, "We may *serve* the living God!" Yet here in Malachi the Lord was forced to ask, "If I am a master, where is the respect due me?" The third kind of disrespect is perhaps the most surprising. The priests themselves placed defiled food on God's altar (verse 7). If the priests themselves showed no respect for the God they claimed to serve, how would the people be led to feel this respect when they worshiped God?

In our day and age of so many charlatans in pulpits, we especially understand the Lord's concern. Matthew 15:14 tells us, "If a blind man leads a blind man, both will fall into a pit." If a priest is blind as to what is a good gift to offer God, then people will also be. Because of disrespect, the Lord said to the priests, "I am not pleased with you . . . and I will accept no offering from your hands."

The gift of the hand is determined worthy by the heart. Mud pies are acceptable to the Lord if given from a childlike heart of love that sees them as beautiful. Consider the woman who offered her small coins in the New Testament! On the other hand, the best gift given with the idea that it limps (but God won't care) will cause the Lord to say, "I am not pleased with you, and I will accept no offering from your hands."

There is an easy way to tell if a gift is going to be acceptable to the Lord. Does it make the heart of the giver beat faster to give it? Does it seem good to the giver? Would he like to receive such a gift himself? Is he happy with the gift, even to the point of causing his old nature to cry out that the gift is too big and too good? This is the way it is in the realm of love and gift giving. Love gives exorbitant gifts! And it insists on this!

The Lord spoke against crippled, diseased, and useless worship. The gift must fit the name. Verses 11 and 14 say, "My name will be great among the nations. . . . For I am a great king . . . and my name is to be feared among the nations." Disrespectful giving takes the Lord's name in vain and thereby breaks the Second Commandment.

Admonition for the priests

2 "And now this admonition is for you, O priests. [2]If you do not listen, and if you do not set your heart to honor my name," says the LORD Almighty, "I will send a curse upon you, and I will curse your blessings. Yes, I have already cursed them, because you have not set your heart to honor me.

[3]"Because of you I will rebuke your descendants; I will spread on your faces the offal from your festival sacrifices, and you will be carried off with it. [4]And you will know that I have sent you this admonition so that my covenant with Levi may continue," says the LORD Almighty. [5]"My covenant was with him, a covenant of life and peace, and I gave them to him; this called for reverence and he revered me and stood in awe of my name. [6]True instruction was in his mouth and nothing false was found on his lips. He walked with me in peace and uprightness, and turned many from sin.

[7]"For the lips of a priest ought to preserve knowledge, and from his mouth men should seek instruction—because he is the messenger of the LORD Almighty. [8]But you have turned from the way and by your teaching have caused many to stumble; you have violated the covenant with Levi," says the LORD Almighty. [9]"So I have caused you to be despised and humiliated before all the people, because you have not followed my ways but have shown partiality in matters of the law."

In the Old Testament the priests were the mediators between a sinful people and the holy God.

Priests received no preferential treatment from the one they claim as Lord for themselves and the one they proclaimed as Lord to their people.

That is clear in this section. In fact, the sin of the priests was especially grievous to the Lord because it led the people astray. "To whom much has been given, much will be expected" is an often stated axiom from the Bible. Much was given to the priests. They were under special covenant with the Lord, the covenant established with Levi. They were chosen and equipped to be leaders (for whom God calls to lead, he equips to lead). Verse 7 states God's expectations: "The lips of a priest ought to preserve knowledge, and from his mouth men should seek instruction." But the priests did not live up to the high honor of their calling, and God was angry.

Priests who approached their work in a flippant way ("you do not set your heart to honor my name") not only brought trouble to themselves, but they also hurt the people. The priests, according to the covenant, were to bless the people. God said to Moses, "Tell Aaron and his sons, 'This is how you are to bless the Israelites. Say to them: "The LORD bless you and keep you; the LORD make his face shine upon you and be gracious to you; the LORD turn his face toward you and give you peace." ' So they will put my name on the Israelites, and I will bless them" (Numbers 6:23-27). But this was not happening, nor would it happen because of a dishonoring of God's name on the part of the priests. The blessing was turned into a curse.

The dynamite of God's blessing is not defused because of evil men. It is possible, for instance, for people to receive blessing from a sacrament administered by an unbeliever.

The efficacy of the blessing does not depend on the faith of the person administering it. The valid check of God's blessings is never returned because of "insufficient funds," regardless of the hand that passes it on—providing it is a valid check in the first place, providing it comes from God and his Word and revelation.

But people *are* cursed by hollow-hearted leaders who pretend to bless them and by priests who are not for the Lord but against him (and remember that those are the only two options). Then it is not God's blessing that is being cursed but the blessing of the person giving it. The Lord here says, "I will curse your blessings." Then the blessing truly "bounces," and it has stamped "insufficient funds" all over it.

The people were cursed in believing they had a blessing when they didn't. It was bogus; it was a curse. If the priest withdrew himself from the spiritual employ of his Master by his disregard of the First Commandment (a failure to revere God and stand in awe of his name—"fear, love, and trust in God above all things"), he also gave up his right to pass along God's blessings.

It is a comfort to know that the Lord of the church deals with his workers. Who besides him knows their hearts? Who besides him can come to them with this charge: "You do not set your heart to honor my name"? And he makes his threat stand: "Because of you I will rebuke [or 'cut off'] your descendants." The Lord of the church sooner or later reveals the false priests for what they truly are: "I have caused you to be despised and humiliated before all the people."

He who knows everything comes to his priests with the statement of his divine intention: "I have sent you this admonition so that my covenant with Levi may continue." The priesthood, the ministry, lives on with faithful workers because the Lord sees to it and makes it continue. His expectations in verse 7 are met in workers he calls and sends and stands behind. Knowledge is preserved and passed down; true instruction, as Levi gave, continues to be given.

Judah unfaithful

¹⁰Have we not all one Father? Did not one God create us? Why do we profane the covenant of our fathers by breaking faith with one another?

¹¹Judah has broken faith. A detestable thing has been committed in Israel and in Jerusalem: Judah has desecrated the sanctuary the LORD loves, by marrying the daughter of a foreign god. ¹²As for the man who does this, whoever he may be, may the LORD cut him off from the tents of Jacob—even though he brings offerings to the LORD Almighty.

¹³Another thing you do: You flood the LORD's altar with tears. You weep and wail because he no longer pays attention to your offerings or accepts them with pleasure from your hands. ¹⁴You ask, "Why?" It is because the LORD is acting as the witness between you and the wife of your youth, because you have broken faith with her, though she is your partner, the wife of your marriage covenant.

¹⁵Has not the LORD made them one? In flesh and spirit they are his. And why one? Because he was seeking godly offspring. So guard yourself in your spirit, and do not break faith with the wife of your youth.

¹⁶"I hate divorce," says the LORD God of Israel, "and I hate a man's covering himself with violence as well as with his garment," says the LORD Almighty.

So guard yourself in your spirit, and do not break faith.

Verse 10 sets the theme question for the following verses: Did not God create us, and if he did, shouldn't we be faithful to him and to each other?

In Scripture time and again God is portrayed as the faithful one in a relationship, the one who holds to his promise. Think of the times we read, "I am the God of your fathers, of Abraham and Isaac and Jacob." His record for keeping his promises is impeccable in his dealings with our fathers. Think of the times we hear, "This happened that the Scripture might be fulfilled." He is faithful to what he has said. In 2 Timothy 2:13 Paul maintained, "If we are faithless, he will remain faithful, for he cannot disown himself." God is faithful and true, and he wants these to be characteristics of his people too.

Unfaithfulness shows its ugly face on two occasions. The first is that awful unfaithfulness when there is flirting with a foreign god. Judah is accused of this. "Judah has broken faith, . . . has desecrated the sanctuary the Lord loves, by marrying the daughter of a foreign god." This sin, spiritual adultery, is against the First Commandment. And adultery polluted the temple of God. It affected the church and still does. That "daughter of a foreign god" today might well be the almighty dollar or prestige in the eyes of the world. As a result of this adultery, prayers were not heard and offerings were not received, as Malachi the prophet stated.

The heart has to be right before the worship is right. God wants true love, not polluted love. Actions and words do not mean anything to the Lord if they are not guided by the undivided attention that true love gives.

The Lord sees through the crocodile tears too, those that "flood the Lord's altar." "Why?" is the question. "It seems that God doesn't hear my prayers anymore." Could it be that God is not hearing the prayers of people today for the same reason that he no longer heard the prayers of his people in Malachi's day? Love has gone bad!

The Lord looks upon his people as his beloved wife. He did it in Malachi's day; he still does it today. "As a bridegroom rejoices over his bride, so will your God rejoice over you" (Isaiah 62:5). It isn't hard to see that this tender, beautiful marriage relationship he established in a perfect, pre-sin world is something he especially values and wants to protect. Faithfulness to a marriage partner is a reflection of the marriage God wants to exist between himself and his people. He has always been faithful to his people in his marriage to them. He wants them, in turn, to be faithful to each other in their own individual marriages.

Broken marriage is broken trust. As such, it stands as a blatant monument for everyone to see that human beings are unable and unwilling to be faithful. It is a wailing and lamenting witness to the failure of two people to keep their word.

Our world has grown calloused to divorce. Divorce and its accompanying evils are painted today as not so bad. In fact, they are considered by many the honorable (or at least necessary) way out for people who valiantly tried but just couldn't make it work. It can even be made to have a nice ring to it when said in just the right way. But the God who does not change (see 3:6) says, "I hate divorce." He has not changed in his feeling. If the morals of people change, God's have not. If we who now read Malachi's words have somehow lost our horror over the fact that divorce is presently a one in two statistic in marriages in the country we call home, let us all be assured that God is still horrified. It is a terrible thing when people do something that God hates.

Verse 15 points to the fact that in marriage a man and his wife are made one in body and in spirit. "They will become one flesh," God said in Genesis 2:24. The unity is also one of spirit: "So guard yourself *in your spirit,* and do not break faith with the wife of your youth." The spirit is intimately affected by any breech of faith in the body. Actually, the faithlessness that may take place in a physical way comes as the result of a faithless spirit. So the man and his wife are one, body and soul.

Now comes the question "Why one?" The Lord answers with this statement: "Because [God] was seeking godly offspring."

There have been different interpretations of this statement, but one interpretation is most obvious. The Lord said at the time of the first marriage, "Be fruitful and increase in number" (Genesis 1:28). There is no question that the Lord blessed the first marriage with children and still wants to bless marriage with children. There is also no question as to what he wants a married couple to do with their offspring. "Bring them up in the training and instruction of the Lord" (Ephesians 6:4). The home is the greenhouse for future Christian plants "because he was seeking godly offspring."

We certainly see and feel the havoc wreaked in homes by divorce, and we realize that when this happens Christian instruction is frequently one of the first things to suffer. There no longer is a father to sit at the table with the catechism and instruct his family as Martin Luther rightfully envisioned it when he formulated the catechism. Besides this, what chance do children have of being godly offspring after they have witnessed the selfishness, lovelessness, inability to forgive, unfaithfulness, and refusal to sacrifice inherently in divorce? For parents to raise up godly offspring, it has to be more than "Do as I say, not as I do." The Lord hates divorce. We should too. Look at what it does! Hear what it says!

Unfaithfulness is a matter of violence. Right along with the Lord's statement "I hate divorce" we read, "I hate a man's covering himself with violence as well as with his garment." Think of the violence caused to a home, feelings, love, children, and peace by one moment's unfaithfulness.

To be unfaithful to a promise is to be a violent person, to wrench, ruin, and destroy.

The Hebrew word for *divorce* is the word that means "to send away." The Lord hates divorce, yet he too will divorce some. He will send them away. It will be the ultimate in divorce when the Lord finally says, "Depart from me, you evildoers. I was faithful to you, but you insisted on being unfaithful to me. I wanted to forgive you and take you back again. Time and again I wanted it, but you wouldn't have it. Now, depart forever!"

This thought brings shivers of fear. We all have been guilty of spiritual unfaithfulness. Every time we break the First Commandment and allow something to pass seductively between us and God, we prove unfaithful. Yet we come back to the Lord's Word in 2 Timothy 2:13: "If we are faithless, he will remain faithful, for he cannot disown himself."

Broken promises can be healed by forgiveness. The Lord Jesus looks at us and says, "I do not condemn you, but go and sin no more." He said that to the woman caught in the act of adultery (John 8:11). And to the Samaritan woman by the well who had five husbands and was living with a man who was not her husband, Jesus said, "[You] must worship in spirit and in truth" (John 4:24). God is true in what he says and does; he wants us to be true too.

"So guard yourself in your spirit, and do not break faith."

The day of judgment

[17]You have wearied the LORD with your words.

"How have we wearied him?" you ask. By saying, "All who do evil are good in the eyes of the LORD, and he is pleased with them" or "Where is the God of justice?"

3 "See, I will send my messenger, who will prepare the way before me. Then suddenly the Lord you are seeking will come to his temple; the messenger of the covenant, whom you desire, will come," says the LORD Almighty.

²But who can endure the day of his coming? Who can stand when he appears? For he will be like a refiner's fire or a launderer's soap. ³He will sit as a refiner and purifier of silver; he will purify the Levites and refine them like gold and silver. Then the LORD will have men who will bring offerings in righteousness, ⁴and the offerings of Judah and Jerusalem will be acceptable to the LORD, as in days gone by, as in former years.

⁵"So I will come near to you for judgment. I will be quick to testify against sorcerers, adulterers and perjurers, against those who defraud laborers of their wages, who oppress the widows and the fatherless, and deprive aliens of justice, but do not fear me," says the LORD Almighty.

The closing verse of chapter 2 presents us with an impossibility—God getting tired. But there is one thing that makes the Almighty tired. He gets tired when his people complain, whine, and accuse him unjustly. They say that he is a God who loves evildoers!

Nothing could be farther from the truth, but that is the blasphemous conclusion made by people who judge things around them and decide that because the evil people flourish and God's people suffer, God must love the evil more than the good. The writer of Psalm 73 came to this same conclusion: "I envied the arrogant when I saw the prosperity of the wicked. They have no struggles; their bodies are healthy and strong. They are free from the burdens common to man; they are not plagued by human ills. This is what the wicked are like—always carefree, they increase in wealth" (verses 3-5,12). The wicked plays; God's favorite sits on the ash heap scraping his boils with a scrap of pottery.

God is not fair! And the omnipotent God sighs in weariness when he hears it. Judgment is coming and it is coming quickly, like the lightning that always takes its victims by surprise. The same overpowering right, light, and power of the lightning is God's judgment. "For as lightning that comes from the east and is visible even in the west, so will be the coming of the Son of Man" (Matthew 24:27). Who will be able to stand it?

Jesus' coming at the first Christmas took people by surprise. Mary, Joseph, Herod, shepherds, friends, and enemies—all were surprised when he came. God had promised his Son's coming from the dawn of the world; people had carried the thought and hope with them through all the long years, but what they hoped for they really did not expect. It caught them by surprise. And the second coming of this "desired" One will also surprise us, even though we hope for it and profess to long for it.

"How long?" the saints in heaven cry to the Lord of judgment. The messengers have proceeded on the pavement of time. Their voices have echoed down into the little corners of this world. John the Baptist called out of the coming day of judgment. "You brood of vipers! Who warned you to flee from the coming wrath?" he said (Luke 3:7). Jesus, God's greatest messenger, spoke of earthquakes and famines, love growing cold, and "great distress," unequaled from the beginning of the world until now—and never to be equaled again" (Matthew 24:21). The day of God's judgment is coming all right! Jesus, the messenger of the covenant whom we desire, has spoken.

The question is, Who will be able to endure that day? Who will be able to stand? Certainly even the hearts of the elect of God will melt like gold in the fire. Self-reliant, strong knees will buckle and sag as the righteous God approaches. The phrase "Who can endure?" literally stated says, "Who can take this in?" Who can comprehend what is going to happen, the process that must be completed before

God's children stand pure and holy before his throne to begin the eternal celebrations?

Malachi presents us with different pictures of the cleansing used to prepare for this day. The refining of heat is one. This hymn verse comes to mind:

> When through fiery trials thy pathway shall lie,
> My grace, all-sufficient, shall be thy supply.
> The flames shall not hurt thee; I only design
> Thy dross to consume and thy gold to refine.
>
> (TLH 427:5)

The picture of a launderer is also used, one who cleans by rubbing, kneading, and beating to make cloth soft, clean, and pliable. This is the old-ribbed-washboard School of Hard Knocks in which God makes his children bend easily and quickly to his will. There is also the picture of sweeping clean with a broom. "His winnowing fork is in his hand, and he will clear his threshing floor, gathering his wheat into the barn and burning up the chaff with unquenchable fire" (Matthew 3:12). John the Baptist said these words, and he prefaced them by saying, "He will baptize you with the Holy Spirit and with fire" (Luke 3:16). The prophet Malachi used the idea of a sieve. This was a skin like that of the chamois that was used to filter out impurities from liquid, a practice that is still done in third world countries today to remove the impurities from diesel fuel.

The Lord desires a pure product. "You shall be holy because your God is holy" is a theme played often in the Bible. We can't even be 99-and-a-large-fraction-percent clean. But who can stand if that is the case? Who can bring his offerings to God knowing that he is completely, one hundred-percent pure?

The answer is, God's people can. They have in the past; they do in the present; they will in the future and on that great day when he comes. "The sacrifices of God are a broken spirit" (Psalm 51:17), and "the offerings of Judah and Jerusalem will be acceptable to the LORD, as in days gone by, as in former years." The heart that desires to be scrubbed and scoured clean by the blood of Jesus, the heart encased in the armor of God, stands! "Therefore put on the full armor of God, so that when the day of evil comes, you may be able to stand your ground, and after you have done everything, to stand" (Ephesians 6:13). "Create in me a pure heart, O God, and renew a steadfast spirit within me" (Psalm 51:10). These words of David were not said wistfully but certainly—positively.

Verse 5 closes this section by reminding God's people that he is the God who judges those intent on covering up the truth with a lie—sorcerers in the field of religion, adulterers in human relationships, perjurers in courts. He also is the God of the underdog, championing the cause of the defenseless—the laborers, the widows, the fatherless, the aliens. He calls the wicked to justice because they do not fear him; it is this very lack of fear that makes them bold to perpetrate their lies and their evil deeds. They will hear this verdict: contempt of court, contempt of the First Commandment.

Robbing God

⁶"I the LORD do not change. So you, O descendants of Jacob, are not destroyed. ⁷Ever since the time of your forefathers you have turned away from my decrees and have not kept them. Return to me, and I will return to you," says the LORD Almighty.

"But you ask, 'How are we to return?'

⁸"Will a man rob God? Yet you rob me.

"But you ask, 'How do we rob you?'

"In tithes and offerings. ⁹You are under a curse—the whole nation of you—because you are robbing me. ¹⁰Bring the whole tithe into the storehouse, that there may be food in my house. Test me in this," says the LORD Almighty, "and see if I will not throw open the floodgates of heaven and pour out so much blessing that you will not have room enough for it. ¹¹I will prevent pests from devouring your crops, and the vines in your fields will not cast their fruit," says the LORD Almighty. ¹²"Then all the nations will call you blessed, for yours will be a delightful land," says the LORD Almighty.

The Lord does not change. This is at the beginning of the admonition to give. This is paramount to the discussion of giving—whether it comes to Malachi's people in the Old Testament or to believers living in New Testament times. God does not change, and he couples this thought with another thought equally important to our understanding of his command to give: "So you, O descendants of Jacob, are not destroyed." God's goodness and preservation are not dependent on our giving, as if they trickled through the meter of our giving to him. His mercies to us are new every morning. Because of this, God's people are not destroyed. If he did give in proportion to their giving to him, they would most certainly perish.

He does have words with his people, however. "You are robbing me." The accusation flabbergasted the people. "How?" they asked incredulously. The answer to how God's people robbed (and still rob) him was in their giving. Giving and loving are really synonymous.

God's complaint was not over money—as if he needed his people's money!—but over what the giving of that money demonstrated—*love!*

A curse followed. "If anyone does not love the Lord—a curse be on him," the apostle Paul warned (1 Corinthians 16:22). God's people were not destroyed, but they lived under a curse. Life was not what it should have been, not what their Lord would have intended if their giving was in right step to the beat of their love for him. What the Lord wanted and planned for them was riches and wild surplus. When he said "Test me . . . and see," he knew the answer and action he was going to give. Pests would flee, crops would flourish, and the land would be a delight to live in.

The Lord God does not change! Even though this is in the Old Testament, it comes from a God who does not change. He gives his people their lives and the accessories that go along with those lives. He still acts in love to his people; he still wants them to act in love to him. The law of the tithe has been lifted (see Colossians 2:16,17), but the law of love has not. And love demands disciplined giving. That is one way we deal with our old natures. The changeless God still instructs his people to "run the race." They are to "keep under [their bodies]" (1 Corinthians 9:27 KJV); they are to "fight the good fight" (1 Timothy 6:12). He instructs them "to get rid of" evil desires (James 1:21; Ephesians 4:31). He instructs his people to live disciplined and measured lives to keep them free from "the sin that so easily entangles" (Hebrews 12:1).

Malachi's people lived with the law of the tithe. God's New Testament people do not. Certainly today the changeless God does not command that each of his people gives a certain amount, but he *does* demand that each determines how much he is going to give and then gives! "On the first day of every week, each one of you should set aside a sum of money in keeping with his income, saving it up, so that when I come no collections will have to be made" (1 Corinthians 16:2).

> ¹³"You have said harsh things against me," says the LORD.
> "Yet you ask, 'What have we said against you?'
> ¹⁴"You have said, 'It is futile to serve God. What did we gain by carrying out his requirements and going about like mourners

before the LORD Almighty? ¹⁵But now we call the arrogant blessed. Certainly the evildoers prosper, and even those who challenge God escape.'"

¹⁶Then those who feared the LORD talked with each other, and the LORD listened and heard. A scroll of remembrance was written in his presence concerning those who feared the LORD and honored his name.

¹⁷"They will be mine," says the LORD Almighty, "in the day when I make up my treasured possession. I will spare them, just as in compassion a man spares his son who serves him. ¹⁸And you will again see the distinction between the righteous and the wicked, between those who serve God and those who do not.

So we come to the last example of the divine/human repartee that the book of Malachi is famous for. People have said harsh things to God, and they have the impudence to ask, "How have we done it? What have we said?"

The complaint that God's people of any age are tempted to issue is that God is not fair. How, for instance, in sacred history could a God of right let his servant Naboth be stoned to death and robbed of possessions by the wicked woman Jezebel? Yet it happened. How, in fact, could a righteous God allow evil men to triumph over his Son, Jesus, and bludgeon him to a cross? It too happened. And in either case, at the time the fairness was not evident. But God's ways continue to not be our ways, and his thoughts not our thoughts. We may not see the fairness—there *may not be* fairness! Sin is never fair. It always goes against God's justice. The miracle is that through the unfairness is a way, and God's ways are always right!

The Lord's promise to all of his children is, "In this world you will have trouble. But take heart! I have overcome the world" (John 16:33). As mentioned earlier, the psalmist Asaph complained with Malachi's people: "They [the wicked] have no struggles; their bodies are healthy and strong. They are free from the burdens common to man;

they are not plagued by human ills" (Psalm 73:4,5). But he spoke further: "When I tried to understand all this, it was oppressive to me till I entered the sanctuary of God; then I understood their final destiny" (verses 16,17). And he closed his psalm with these words: "Those who are far from you will perish; you destroy all who are unfaithful to you. But as for me, it is good to be near God. I have made the Sovereign LORD my refuge; I will tell of all your deeds" (verses 27,28).

In comparing Asaph's words above with the words in Malachi 3:14,15, we see that the complaint was really the same. And the complaint still surfaces today with statements like this: "How can a fair God allow that to happen?" The prophet Ezekiel gives us one final commentary on man's challenging God's fairness: "Your countrymen say, 'The way of the Lord is not just.' But it is their way that is not just. If a righteous man turns from his righteousness and does evil, he will die for it. And if a wicked man turns away from his wickedness and does what is just and right, he will live by doing so. Yet, O house of Israel, you say, 'The way of the Lord is not just.' But I will judge each of you according to his own ways" (Ezekiel 33:17-20).

The answer to this whole unfair discussion—on unfairness!—is simply, "The Lord *is* fair!" Judgment day will be the grand final show of God's fairness. No one will be able to contest the outcome of that day. In verse 17 God promises to act fairly to his treasured possession "in the day." Many things that now stand on the fringe of people's understanding of God's fairness will be cleared up then. The distinction mentioned in verse 18 will be seen then, the distinction made by the Judge with his final "come" and "depart."

There will be compassion in the voice of the Judge when he says, "Come, blessed of my Father, inherit the kingdom prepared for you." And verse 17 will most certainly be fulfilled: "They will be mine . . . I will spare them, just as in compassion a man spares his son who serves him." The sons all come home. They are safe.

The word here for "compassion" is the same word used in Hebrew to describe Pharaoh's daughter's feelings as she peered into the little, pitched ark and saw crying baby Moses. How comforting to have a God of compassion! "For we do not have a high priest who is unable to sympathize with our weaknesses" (Hebrews 4:15). The sympathy comes because God is our Father, as he points out in verse 17. He feels for us because we are his. Isaiah 49:15 points to the strongest kind of love we know: "Can a mother forget the baby at her breast and have no compassion on the child she has borne? Though she may forget, I will not forget you!" There is something stronger than a mother's love! There is the Father's love—the kind described by God for us, his children.

As we approach the last chapter of the Old Testament and the final revelation of God to his people for almost four hundred years, we read what the prophet said about the Father and his children. Malachi spoke about the end of time, when the Father would come and right all wrongs and receive all children whom he loved and who served him.

The day of the Lord

4 **"Surely the day is coming; it will burn like a furnace. All the arrogant and every evildoer will be stubble, and that day that is coming will set them on fire," says the Lord Almighty. "Not a root or a branch will be left to them. 2But for you who revere my name, the sun of righteousness will rise with healing in its wings. And you will go out and leap like calves released from the stall. 3Then you will trample down the wicked; they will be ashes under the soles of your feet on the day when I do these things," says the Lord Almighty.**

4"Remember the law of my servant Moses, the decrees and laws I gave him at Horeb for all Israel.

⁵"See, I will send you the prophet Elijah before that great and dreadful day of the LORD comes. ⁶He will turn the hearts of the fathers to their children, and the hearts of the children to their fathers; or else I will come and strike the land with a curse."

The last chapter of the Old Testament talks about the "coming" day. It is a day of wild extremes. The wicked are like chaff, swept away in engulfing flames. When the fire is past, nothing remains but ashes, their place knows them no more. "Not a root or a branch will be left to them." On the other hand, the Sun of righteousness will rise above the horizon. The believers have been looking. There has long been a glow in the sky. They know the sun is coming. Those in darkness have seen a great light. Now it peeps above the horizon and leaps into the sky in all its splendor. It brings healing too. We bask our cold stiff joints and limbs—and hearts—in its glow. It heals and restores. It brings life eternal life!

Besides this wonderful, warming Sun (and we could also spell that S-o-n if we wanted to) there is the picture of calves released from their stalls after being penned up all winter. They feel good. They want to run and jump for the sheer joy of it. That's the way it is with Christ's people, who understand and appreciate that Christ has set them free.

No sick calf feels like jumping. The sickness of sin is past! Our spirits *feel* good! They want to kick and frolic in God's sunshine forever—and they shall! Nothing can hold them back. Imagine racing up the slopes of light! The saints stream into their final pasture. The Good Shepherd has kept his word. All is well and good.

God's good name is involved here as well. And this too is pastoral, coming from the Good Shepherd chapter of the Bible (John 10). There Jesus says, "I know my sheep and my sheep know me. I have other sheep that are not of this sheep pen. I must bring them also. They too will listen to my voice, and there shall be one flock and one shepherd" (verses 14,16). We know God's name. And Philippians 2:10 says, "At the *name of Jesus* every knee should bow, in heaven and on earth and under the earth, and every tongue confess that Jesus Christ is Lord, to the glory of God the Father."

Verse 4 mentions the law. This is the word *torah*. It comes from the verb meaning "to teach" or "to instruct." Here it does not mean just the laws with dos and do nots but also, and especially, the words of promise and instruction, the complete revelation of God to his people. We are saved through this revelation of God's will, this instruction. It was something good. "Do this and you will live" (Luke 10:28). This was the manual for life, the manual to life. We are saved by the Word and through the Word. Here at the end of the Old Testament, God's people were asked to remember. Remember the rules. Remember the umpire's decision, the blueprints for life.

What a treasure we have in our hands. We can search through the will of God as a lawyer ruffles through a dossier or a student looks through a notebook. God gave his people his plan for life. How happy the devil is when they neglect it. How sad he is when God's people make faithful use of it. How close we all are to the Last Day and to judgment.

The prophet Elijah was promised to the Old Testament people. Jesus commented on this in Matthew 17:11-13: "'To be sure, Elijah comes and will restore all things. But I tell you, Elijah has already come, and they did not recognize him, but have done to him everything they wished. In the same way the Son of Man is going to suffer at their hands.' Then the disciples understood that he was talking to them about John the Baptist." And what Luke wrote in chapter

1:17 draws us even closer to these last words of Malachi: "He [John] will go on before the Lord, in the spirit and power of Elijah, to turn the hearts of the fathers to their children and the disobedient to the wisdom of the righteous—to make ready a people prepared for the Lord." These are the very words Malachi wrote in verse 6.

The Word speaks in other places about how, as the world nears its end, children will turn against their parents and parents will turn against their children. Our world is full of examples that this happens and is happening. Parents commit the ultimate in child abuse—they neglect their children's souls. They don't care where their children will spend eternity. They spend money for their children's bodies and for their education, but they neglect to tell the children the commands and laws of God, to talk about them on the way, to write them in their homes and on their hearts.

But there is also the fact that as the day grows closer and closer, fathers and children will be talking to each other and turning to each other. There will be good families. God will see to it! In our day when we sometimes feel like despairing because there are no good families left, there *are* good families. Families *do* pray together and *do* stay together through life. This is the greatest turning together of hearts, fathers talking to their children about the Savior, children talking to their fathers. Their hearts are touched through the only thing that touches hearts, the Word of God.

Here, at the very end of the Old Testament, there is a reference to Christian education. It is not only education of a formal nature in classrooms but the education that comes from hearts that really and truly care for each other. Education—heart to heart! From fathers to their children!

If it is not this, then comes a curse. In the English Bible, the Old Testament ends with the word *curse.* Homiletics professors do not teach their students to end their sermons with the word *curse*. This did not seem to be a good way to end the Old Testament and to leave the people hanging for the next four hundred years before the babe of Bethlehem arrived in swaddling clothes.

It is a somber way to end, but Malachi's words are meant to draw us up short. They were spoken in the spirit of the prophets, of whom Malachi was the last. Judgment is coming, but with this "great and dreadful day of the Lord" there is also hope and coming salvation. We wait for it. We peer into the future as Malachi and his people did, hands shading our eyes as we scan the horizon. We are millennia closer to that day!

Even so, come quickly, Lord Jesus!

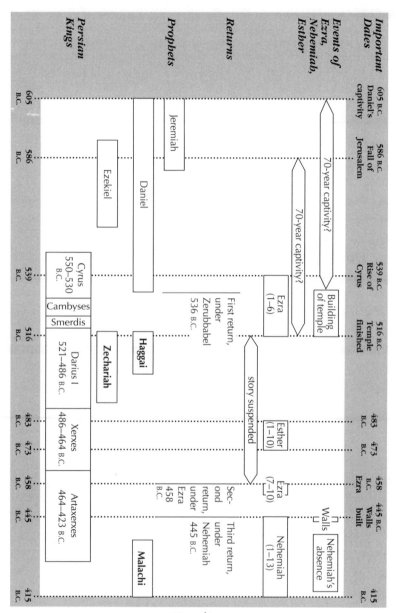

Timeline